R. M. PELUSO

deep
tasting

CHOCOLATE & WHISKEY

Ritual
Communications
New York

Published by Ritual Communications
Copyright © 2017 by R. M. Peluso

For information contact: Ritual Communications
www.ritualcommunications.com

Library of Congress Cataloging-in-Publication Data is available
ISBN   978-0-9794674-6-2 (ebook)
ISBN   978-0-9794674-7-9 (paperback)

Cover, text design and photo editing by Lisa Hayden-Miller
lisa@photomagicdesigns.com

Photo by Serge Gree Photography and Videography,
New York

Contents

Praise for *Deep Tasting Chocolate & Whiskey*

A thoroughly researched and analytical approach to finding the harmonies in two gustatory luxuries – whisky and chocolate. By deconstructing and detailing the essences of the two, R. M. Peluso explains how and why their similar and contrasting flavors can work in synergy to achieve some dazzling pairings.
—Davin de Kergommeaux, author,
Canadian Whisky: The New Portable Expert

The pleasure of tasting a specific food requires a meditative concentration that particularly suits the appreciation of chocolate and whiskey as R. M. Peluso so well describes. I have struggled happily with similar combinations and have discovered many wonderful flavor surprises. These likewise await the readers of *Deep Tasting Chocolate & Whiskey*.
—John Scharffenberger, co-founder,
Scharffen Berger Chocolate Maker

The honest truth is, we don't often think of pairing whiskey with food. Unlike wine, it's a challenge to match up the flavors and experience in many cases. The one exception is always...chocolate. Chocolate is a signature flavor note in single malt whiskey in particular, like we make here at Westland. The rich malty notes from the grain and the sweetness from our casks is complemented well

by the right chocolate, accentuating both in the process. R. M. Peluso shows us precisely how to select the most compatible partners.
—Matt Hoffman, Master Distiller, Westland Distillery

R. M. Peluso's well researched *Deep Tasting Chocolate & Whiskey* offers readers a delicious and comprehensive guide to the nature of my favorite two things. For the chocolate and whiskey geeks there are descriptions, selection guides for both and even technical charts. And for the simple chocolate lover like me, the obscure information included about from where and how our favorite chocolates come to be will come in handy next time my chocolate jag strikes. I highly recommend the ganache and truffles recipes with rye whiskey. They come with guaranteed standing ovation when you put them out for dessert with a dram of whiskey.
—Ralph Erenzo, co-founder, Tuthilltown Spirits LLC

Praise for *Deep Tasting: A Chocolate Lover's Guide to Meditation*

As a chocolate maker, I was happy with the level of detail in this book about the chocolate making process. But as a long time meditator, I was thrilled to see the possibilities of the nexus of mindfulness and chocolate. R. M. Peluso takes her readers to a level of tasting that is beyond any other I've seen before. I look forward to trying this meditation technique myself and expect full on theta waves. I learned a lot about tasting chocolate and am sure you will too!
—Shawn Askinosie, Founder & CEO, Askinosie Chocolate

This absorbing book is a unique and fascinating guide to the taste, aroma, and even the making of fine artisanal (single origin) chocolate, "from bean-to-bar." Whether one is or is not a follower of the meditation path described by the author, all chocolate lovers will learn much from this delightful and instructive read. Highly recommended!

—Michael D. Coe, author *The Maya*; co-author,
The True History of Chocolate

In my book, I wrote that the most important thing to bring to a chocolate tasting is a sense of humor. After reading *Deep Tasting: A Chocolate Lover's Guide to Meditation*, I would have to say that mindfulness can also be valuable. I started using chocolate, consciously, as a tool to focus attention during my meditation exercises and I found that it allowed me to calm my mind, and filter out distractions, faster than when not using chocolate. Chocolate is going to be a part of my regular meditation routine from now on!

—Clay Gordon, author, *Discover Chocolate*

R. M. Peluso has created a well-written memoir that provides a path to meditation using chocolate as a spiritual medium. I'd been considering meditation as a way of relaxing and managing stress, but, oddly enough, I'd never thought about chocolate as my medium. Dr. Peluso's book is a very enjoyable read that covers the key historical and cultural significances of cacao while also chronicling her own journey to making chocolate from the bean. The book serves as a detailed sensory tasting guide that's essential for any serious chocolate taster, and it should be required reading for anyone making chocolate from the bean.

—Lauren Adler, Chocolopolis, Seattle

I looked forward to R.M.'s book as I knew she would bring a new approach to the discussion of why we love chocolate so much and the importance of understanding chocolate flavor. She didn't disappoint, and her love of chocolate comes through on every page. Yes, the rapid growth in the number of bean-to-bar chocolate makers in the past 10 years means many more choices are available to consumers when they reach for a chocolate bar. And those makers who are smart, passionate and using fine flavor beans with meticulous production processes are sure to continue to wow us with their flavor and quality. For those who practice meditation or are exploring it, her chocolate meditation exercises will be a real treat. I appreciate the exercises as they align totally with our Ecole Chocolat philosophy of mindful, conscious tasting that is taught in all our programs and the focus of our chocolate flavor programs. I think anyone who loves chocolate will find this an enlightening and enjoyable read.

—Pam Williams, Founder and President, Ecole Chocolat Professional School of Chocolate Making; co-author, *Raising the Bar: The Future of Fine Chocolate*

Reverend Dr. R. M. Peluso is a contributing editor to the C-spot®, and needless to state, we're proud of our association and grateful for her generous attributions of our small contribution to this book. Other than God, sex, and, maybe, music, chocolate is the most powerful force in the universe. In *Deep Tasting*, R. M. Peluso covers them all. She delivers her homily with none of the snot-snob stuff of cocoa-doodle gurus. Instead, she walks the path with humility, offering insights that are real, practical and actually beneficial. The nib of the matter: meditation and chocolate share several of the same physical and mental health benefits. Dr. Peluso conveys just what mystics, prophets, yogis, and shamans have known for centuries. The practices outlined herein can be life-changing and rewarding. Ergo, this is possibly the most beneficial piece ever written on the subject of chocolate. Nothing hyperbolic in that statement, either. People often ask us for guidance in locating their own personal C-spot. We direct them to the search features in The Chocolate Census on C-spot.com. But likened to an article of faith, those who have found it never have to ask, and those who have to ask probably will never find it. But now there's renewed hope for any seeker, thanks to *Deep Tasting*.

—Mark Christian, founder, The C-spot® :
The Independent Consumer Guide to
Premium Chocolate

Show me how you drink, and I will tell you who you are.
–Emile Peynaud

What you see before you, my friend, is the result
of a lifetime of chocolate.
–Katharine Hepburn

INTRODUCTION

REMEMBER THAT CLASSIC MOVIE in black and white? An elderly gentleman sits in a leather, wingback chair in his study, shelves laden with books. He holds a tumbler of scotch in his hand. Lost in thought after a day of empire-building, he takes a whiff. Then he sets the glass down and picks up a Cuban cigar. He snips off the head with a silver cigar cutter, waves a lighter across the opposite end, puffs a few times, then takes a leisurely drag. Smoke encircles him. He takes a sip of the scotch. He puffs, he sips. In the presence of the moment, he lets go of his day in one breath, allowing whatever insights and inspiration may flow in. He is not one of the MadMen of the post-war era, indulging to the point of soul annihilation. He's not living in frenzied overdrive; there's no unquenchable pleasure-seeking. His life is purposeful, his pleasures measured and simple, yet profound. Let others seek sacred space, golf green, or beach house. He finds restorative pause in his own, self-constructed rituals, time consecrated unto himself. Peace enters through his senses.

Flash forward. Modern life is stressful. Who does not have a need to balance the demands on their time and energy? Who does not have to contend with emotional burdens? The need for reduced stress takes many of us on nature walks. What is it we do on these excursions? We listen, we gaze, we breathe in the scent of turf in the countryside, the parks, the botanical gardens. We feel the sun's warmth on our faces. We suddenly remember how it feels to open our lungs, ribs spread wide, back muscles letting us know how useful they truly are. We experience our physical selves moving through space, alert to the present moment. We take in the hues and scents of flowers. Tree leaves rustle in the wind. A bird calls then flutters off. While our attention is on these things, other matters recede from awareness. We feel slowed, internal chatter silenced. Time seems irrelevant, suspended. Our senses bring us here fully right now. This is the essence of focus, no matter how brief.

Smell and taste can be gateways to such moments, if we learn to truly savor. We can use these perceptual experiences to commune with, and to internally ground ourselves after a day of being pulled in one direction and pushed in another. In book one of the *Deep Tasting Guide*™ series, *A Chocolate Lover's Guide to Meditation*, I introduced the how-to techniques for intensely appreciating fine chocolate. Beyond the great pleasure that is the gift of the cacao tree and all the hands that work its fruit thereafter, you will have glimpsed, through that book, what it might be like to try traditional meditation. In *Deep Tasting Chocolate and Whiskey*, we move from experiencing dark chocolate alone to exploring the aromas and flavors of scotch and other whiskeys, including bourbon and rye. There will be, similarly, opportunities to reexamine your relationship with spirit as well as chocolate. You will gain understanding of the basics for matching outstanding spirits to great chocolates, and, hopefully, you will be able to enjoy these on your own or socially.

I've included over 140 sample pairings in this book. But I don't intend to spoon-feed you. I've read too many books on chocolate, cheese, wine and whiskey that toss out a few sample pairings without giving the reader the keys to good matching. What is it that makes pairings palatable? These books don't tell you. What makes pairings outstanding? They really don't say. We can assume the writers are drawing on their many years of experience, yet without articulating the underlying principles of flavor, they fail to provide the reader with any enduring skills.

You may be an experienced chocolate taster, or a whiskey connoisseur. Or you may be an absolute novice with respect to either. I make no assumptions about your level of experience. I beg your indulgence, if you are highly experienced with either chocolate or whiskey, and you encounter text that addresses the basics of entry-level information. I hope you will find, somewhere within these pages, that which will specifically speak to you. You are invited to seek your own level and to interact with the information provided in this book in your own way. My goal in writing this guide is to empower you to go forward and make your own matches. To accomplish that aim, I researched and tasted over 100 dark chocolate bars, both blends (made from cacao beans from more than one source) and single origins (made from beans of one region, farm cooperative or single estate) and more than 70 whiskeys (Scotch, Irish, French, Japanese, Taiwanese, American, and Canadian).

While whiskeys may pair nicely with milk, white, and flavored chocolates, this book deliberately emphasizes dark chocolate. The main reasons: dark chocolate reflects all the other expressions of chocolate, and there are too many possible combinations of all others for one book. I've included only a few items in the dark-milk chocolate category. Pairing white, milks, bonbons and truffles with whiskeys will become easier once you master the basics of flavor in this book.

In creating my database, I cross-referenced world chocolates with international single malts and blended whiskies, bourbons, ryes, and craft whiskeys, constructed a classification system, and devised a method based on flavor profiles. We will talk more about flavor profiles later in the book. But let me just say to those who are familiar with the term single origin in respect to chocolate, that knowledge of source simply isn't sufficient information to achieve a good pairing. Those who know their way around single origins probably understand that year to year, harvests will vary. Changes in post-harvest processing can alter flavor. Then too, the way one particular chocolate maker roasts their cocoa beans, then refines them, as well as the amount of sugar and any other ingredients added, can make all the difference between one flavor profile manifesting or another showing up. If you have one minor flavor suppressed or potentiated through handling, you end up with flavor keys that don't quite turn in the locks of a supposedly compatible whiskey, even though another batch of the same type of bean, from the same origin may work beautifully. This is why flavor profiles and compatibilities may be guessed but not absolutely assumed based on origin.

One important reference for me has been the C-spot® (c-spot. com), the chocolate website to which I have contributed reviews since its inception. Mark Christian, the site's founder, once told me at the beginning of our work together that a review was only a "snap-shot in time." His words still resonate because they are true. While researching this book, I would check the flavor profiles against what was reported in the reviews for a particular bar made by a particular chocolate maker, then see if the current batches had similar characteristics. Some of the reviews are more than a couple of years old, and the bars have significantly changed. In the final analysis, I had to check and recheck and re-classify the flavor profiles of chocolate bars by the same chocolate makers. But let me also add, that whiskeys change too. For example, Larceny is a bourbon that has picked up a lot of hot, spicy notes recently. I know that because I've read old reviews and discussion threads online and noticed the dissonance. Even though Larceny is classified as a particular type of bourbon, not accounting for the changes could throw off a pairing made on the basis of its former profile.

The universe of spirits is incredibly diverse. Almost every class of spirits merits its own book. In fact, each spirit type already seems to have several books written about them. During my research, I discovered some of the world's most accomplished writers are not novelists, but hard at work in the world of whiskey— Lew Bryson, Fred Minnick, Dave Broom, and Davin De Kergommeaux, to name but a few. If you want to know the fascinating history of whiskey or how various whiskeys are made, I refer you to those expert writers in the field. You will not find pictures of stills, bottles or whiskey barrels in my book. This *Deep Tasting Guide* ™ is about flavor, how to taste, how to moderately consume chocolate and whiskey, and how to achieve sublime chocolate and whiskey pairings. Period.

You could say there are volumes of spirits to read about, as well as to drink. If I were to attempt to write about spirits in general, I'd need extensive knowledge about rum, tequila, gin, vodka, and many others. I would have to write an encyclopedia rather than this simple pairing guide. Therefore, I had to address myself to just one class of spirits that seemed highly compatible with chocolate, yet underserved in the literature.

Most often, people attempt to pair chocolate with wine. But wine pairing with chocolate can be tricky due to the tendencies of their respective tannins to clash. Personally, I'm allergic to sulfites, so I cannot help you with wine anyway. I recommend that you seek out an expert, like my friend Roxanne Browning of exoticchocolatetasting. com. She's a "chocolate sommelier" with respect to wine. I guess you can call me a "whiskey and chocolate sommelier!"

Whiskey is sometimes used in chocolate bonbons. Additionally, in recent years, cocoa nibs (the nut meat of the shelled cacao beans) have been aged in formerly used, or "ex," bourbon barrels to flavor chocolate bars. But seldom has whiskey been selected as a simple accompaniment to plain chocolate bars. That's because it's not a simple matter. The truth is, to successfully match chocolate with any spirit, you need to know both extremely well. I had already spent more than a decade as a taster and reviewer of chocolate for the C-spot®. Now, in order to learn how to pair chocolate with whiskey, I needed a crash-course in the wide, wide world of whiskey. But I've always loved a challenge!

Before we proceed, let's see if we can clarify a few terms. Like the spelling of whiskey. Or is it whisky? People often ask what the difference is. It's just a spelling convention! Well, mainly. Whisky, without the e, is the preferred spelling in Scotland, Canada, Japan, Europe and most other countries. And, by the way, only a whisky made in Scotland can legally call itself scotch. Ireland and the United States spell whiskey with the e. However, when I see "whisky," I tend to think of a single malt barley-based or blended scotch that may contain other grains. On the other hand, when I see the word "whiskey," I tend to think of a corn-dominant bourbon or a rye-based spirit made in the USA, or a barley-based single malt or blend made in Ireland. There are American wheat whiskeys and corn whiskeys, but those are less common.

With the advent of craft distillers, my simplistic, orthographic compartmentalization occasionally breaks down. For example, Deerhammer and other American distillers are now producing single malt spirits made from barley, just like the Scots. Yet, most American single malt producers spell their spirit "whiskey." But some single malt craft distillers may spell their product without the e. That's their prerogative.

So if I seem to change spelling in midstream, look at the country of origin of the spirit I'm discussing. If some producers are bucking the conventions of their own countries, I will simply respect the spelling of their product. Also, if I'm referring to both whisky and whiskey, as in the title of this book, I will spell it "whiskey" as the all-inclusive, and "whiskeys," as the plural form. Unless I'm referring to the plural of whisky, then I will write "whiskies." Does it matter if you spell the spirits whisky or whiskey? No. You won't be arrested for breaking any laws–unless you're spelling while intoxicated.

A word about my modus operandi. This book isn't about promoting any specific brands, although I will let you know those I have particularly enjoyed. So if your preferences don't match my own, please understand that it's due to individual differences in taste. The objective in this book is to identify classes of chocolates and whiskeys that tend to work well together, not individual products. If I mention that a particular chocolate or whiskey is a personal favorite, it's with the intention of being transparent. *It's important for you to know that I'm not paid by any chocolate or whiskey companies to recommend any product in this book.* It is simply difficult to restrain my enthusiasm when encountering an excellent chocolate or whiskey.

Whiskey tasting notes represent my impressions along with those that form a consensus of the most salient descriptors from multiple sources, including those of the distillers. Frankly, noses with superior experience to mine have examined these spirits from every possible angle. And God bless them, these whiskey reviewers are still educating my palate. Distillers' and reviewers' notes can be quite elaborate, and sometimes approach literary value, to put a diplomatic spin on it. Therefore, in the interest of conciseness, I edited...heavily. In terms of chocolate, as well as chocolate and whiskey pairing notes, the final calls were mine. Not all pairings produced descriptive comments, but they had been ranked as "superior" during data collection and, therefore, were worthy of inclusion.

I wanted to make both the chocolates and whiskeys in this book accessible and affordable. As you might guess, an enormous world of choice awaits you, the consumer. That can be intimidating. You want to buy both great chocolates and spirits, and if you wish to pair them in a way that pleases the palate without going broke in the process, some guidelines would be helpful. Hopefully, you will find this book to be a trustworthy guide. We begin our tastings with training exercises of chocolate and whiskey, independently, as well as their potential matches, that are as easy to find as a local liquor or gourmet foods counter. I tried to consider accessibility on a regional basis, too. Imported products can be difficult and expensive to obtain, so I wanted you to have convenient options. Some chocolates may have to be ordered online, if you aren't living in a major city. The good news is that the best craft chocolate makers have online shops, or are represented in online stores. Beyond our inexpensive training bars, with only a few exceptions, the chocolates sell for under $15, as of this writing. Many of the chocolates recommended in this book are award-winning. All the whiskeys recommended are well under $100 US per bottle, with many under $50. Several airline-size 50 ml bottles recommended for the training exercises are under $7 US. They are all highly palatable, and many of the whiskeys in this book are also award-winning. There are no bad whiskeys or bad chocolates recommended in this book, and there are only superior pairings offered. You will, of course, be the ultimate judge and, hopefully, find your own favorites.

Whiskey can be very expensive. And the prices keep rising. One book, by a well- meaning expert, promised advice on selecting beginning whiskey. Unfortunately, most of the recommendations exceeded $140 per bottle. I find that a bit of a financial risk for many of us, particularly beginners, who don't even know what kind of whiskey they like. If you can spend $140 only to find out that you don't like the whiskey, God bless. But most of us don't wish to make too many costly mistakes. So I was determined to find a way that was less risky. Quality and value—I kept these in mind as I researched this book. I wanted to introduce you to a world of rewarding sensory experiences, without placing obstacles in your way. So both chocolate and whiskey matches had to be excellent, reasonably priced, and easily obtainable.

To book publishers, pairings of food and alcohol are currently "sexy," meaning, they think it will sell more books. As a result, writers may feel compelled to include information they really haven't had time to thoroughly research and assimilate. As a word of caution, you may come across the idea that almost all whiskeys go with all chocolate. No, they don't!

I've seen these blanket statements made before by wine experts or cheese experts, as well as whiskey experts. Anyone who speaks in generalities about dark chocolate going with one type of whiskey, milk chocolate with another and white with still another, doesn't know what they're talking about. Not with any depth, anyway. As you will see, dark chocolate is not some monolithic category. Dark chocolates vary enormously from one to another in terms of aromas, flavors, and degree of bitterness and sweetness, among other values. Matching them properly to anything takes know-how and finesse. The same is true of milk chocolate, particularly today, with the recent appearance of dark milk chocolates. The cacao content in these dark milks sometimes reaches as high as 65% (Bonnat) or 68% (Fruition), levels usually reserved for dark chocolate. Dark milks, in particular, may reflect complex flavors, not the usual sugary- sweet, creamy caramel –flavor dominated products associated with commercial milk chocolate. Legally, the cocoa-mass or liquor (the basis of dark chocolate) in milk chocolate can range from as little as 10% (US) to 25% (EU). It has been rare to find mass-produced milks in excess of 35% cacao. Some white chocolates also reflect more complexity than the usual confectionery sugar and milk notes of the industrial brands, due to specialty cocoa butter and artisan processing. So beware of statements, such as "dark chocolate goes with this whiskey." Really? Which specific dark chocolate bars? And how many dark bars did that voice of authority actually study before reaching their conclusion? For this book, over 100 dark bars and over 70 whiskeys were sampled and paired. I set the bar high. The match had to be more than acceptable. On a scale of 1-10, they only made the cut if the pairing rated a 7 or higher.

I selected all the whiskeys in this book to be entry-level. Many can be found in better bars and pubs. There, a dram (or serving), can be purchased without having to take out a second mortgage. I already mentioned that whiskey can be very pricey. Let me give you an example. A 750 ml bottle of fine 10- or 12-year scotch may sell for approximately $50-80. A 15-year bottle from the same line may jump to $130 or more, and an 18-year perhaps $230 or more. Beyond 20 years, you may be spending $1000 or more, easily.

Hopefully, the 18–or 20-year (or older) scotch is complex and superb. It's meant to be thoughtfully tasted and savored. But please consider that tasting two beverages or foods within a short space of time will alter the perception of both. So combining a complex, top-tier whiskey with a chocolate tasting probably makes little sense. That kind of whiskey stands well enough on its own. I certainly wouldn't want to share a 20-year old scotch with any other aromas or flavors whatsoever. An entry-level, or signature expression of any Scotch or American whiskey is a different story, however; the whiskey and the chocolate can certainly stand on their own—or they wouldn't be included among my recommendations! And they may also pleasantly modify your perception of the other. But I insist that it be in a way that is an additive experience. An entry- level whiskey can also tell you whether you like the style of a particular brand and whether that whiskey maker inspires your confidence. If so, you may then be inclined to go on to try other expressions in their line—the older and pricier ones.

Let me give you another example. I have tasted, and included in this book, brands in the Buffalo Trace Distillery line. Buffalo Trace Kentucky Straight Bourbon may be considered an entry-level spirit, but it is award-winning, and stands perfectly on its own. In addition, it is compatible with many chocolates, as you will find out. Also in the Buffalo Trace family is Eagle Rare 10-Year. I love the rich, oaky, mellow flavor of the Eagle Rare. Also an award-winning bourbon, it is scarcely more expensive, and still very affordable. As of this writing, small bottles are still under $50! These are some of the best buys in American whiskey anywhere. You can enjoy it by itself or with chocolate. But I wouldn't recommend that you try to taste a 23-year-old Pappy Van Winkle with chocolate, even if you can get your hands on one. Okay, I did try some outlandish pairings like that for this book. That's called research. On that basis, I can tell you, it's a waste! The same can be said for Scottish counterparts, for example, The Dalmore's more mature and specialized products. The Dalmore entry-level is the 12-year Single Malt Scotch, a superb signature expression in that distiller's line. The Dalmore 12 is delectable on its own, yet mates well with many chocolates, as you will hopefully discover. Having tried several of the older and unique expressions of The Dalmore, I can tell you that spending time with the richness and subtlety of those very special whiskies is a complete experience in itself. Trying to pair a whisky that is so luxurious with anything is not only redundant, but distracting, and probably, a subtractive experience...in my humble opinion. Attempting to pair a chocolate that is superb and complete can also be quite beside the point. But the chocolate, at least at this writing, still won't cost you a week's rent! I wouldn't want to cheat myself of the full experience of an exquisite whiskey by turning my attention to chocolate or vice versa. So you will be guided to begin with a great chocolate, savor it, get to know it–hell, fall in love!–and if you feel inclined, try it with a whiskey that I've found to be more than compatible.

Let me help you get your feet wet, with whiskey, with chocolate, with whiskey and chocolate. Learn which chocolates appeal to you best, with or without a whiskey companion. Learn the kind of whiskey you like. Find out which brands earn your confidence. Then, with or without chocolate, if you want to splurge on exquisitely- crafted, luxurious scotch or other whiskeys–go for it!

1

SUMPTUOUS SAVORING WITHOUT GOING BROKE

Of all the gin joints in all the towns in all the world, she walks into mine
–Rick Blaine, Casablanca

The marketing of anything is full of exploitation and lies and hype.
–Sydney Pollack

ONE BLUSTERY MANHATTAN NIGHT, I took refuge from the stinging cold by climbing a narrow staircase to the mezzanine of the Flatiron Room, a well-known whiskey bar. I had arrived early and had plenty of time to check out the place. A long series of tables were decked in white linens, white placemats, and white coasters bearing the gold-embossed names of the contents held in multiple whiskey glasses. The settings were laid out for about thirty-five people with disposable incomes. How disposable? Well, they had plunked down nearly $400 for the privilege of tasting 5 sample shots of Pappy Van Winkle whiskeys. I'd soon find out that a few had come to entertain important real estate investors. Others were simply afraid to miss out on the hottest thing. Others confided in hushed tones that the exorbitant price tag was actually the cheapest way to satisfy their curiosity 'as to why the Pappy Van Winkle label commanded such a high price—if you could even obtain it at all. Because the real Pappy bottles are rare. Exceedingly rare.

But I smelled hype. I confess to having a pretty good nose for it. Not long ago I called out a company—To'ak— in the chocolate world that scandalized us by pricing a chocolate bar for between two-three hundred dollars. Packaged in a Spanish oak box, it came accoutered with wooden tongs and a good story. But let's face it, Pappy too was marketed through a good story. Legends in the whiskey trade are, well, legendary. Of course, as it turned out, the older issues of Pappy had been dwindling over the years. Think of old whiskeys as antiques. Whiskey aficionados have been drinking the old Pappy stock into extinction or squirreling them away as investments. Only so many made, only so many still sitting in warehouses, climate-regulated pantries, or forgotten in people's attics. Every once in a while, someone discovers one, then uh-oh, little Freddie smashes it to smithereens. One less antique. The younger releases in the Van Winkle line are not considered genuine Pappy at all. Further, it is suspected that the recent issues are being held back to keep supply low and the price high. And this was extending to others in the distiller's line, such as the Weller label. Creative pricing through controlling supply and demand is nothing new. It can be argued that Pappy-mania has even done a lot of good for the American whiskey business, elevating prices— albeit, unevenly– to match imported scotch through the mid-range. And the rarest Pappy approaches rarer, but not the rarest scotch. Meanwhile the To'ak effect, as of this writing, still remains to be seen. Because no other chocolate bars, even ones far superior to those original batches, sell for even a quarter of the price.

But back in the Flatiron Room, in the midst of these prosperous folks, there was I, a teetotaler for most of my life. My only excuse for such expenditure was the researching of my next book–this one–on pairing chocolate with whiskey. I had to learn to drink, or rather, taste whiskey. So, for a wild-few months, I dragged myself from bar to liquor store, to all the free tastings I could find in Manhattan. Like a college student cramming for an exam, I ran from tasting to tasting, snapping photos and scribbling notes, several times a week, sometimes a couple a day, in order to educate my nose and palate about scotch, bourbon and rye. And I, and my liver, got through it by mostly "nosing" (smelling), taking a tiny sip, spitting out the good along with the less agreeable offerings, or clandestinely tossing the better stuff into a flask before slinking off into the night like a thief. I begged samples from generous, sympathetic suppliers. I stalked whiskey ambassadors. Retailers had pity and took me in. Because I had to learn about American whiskey, Irish whiskey, Canadian, French, Japanese, Taiwanese, and even Indian whisky. Whatever possessed me?

Simply this. I'd spent over a decade cultivating my taste buds as a reviewer of chocolate for the C-spot ® before writing my first book, *Deep Tasting: A Chocolate Lover's Guide to Meditation*. For me, fine chocolate was a complete experience in itself, requiring nothing else. Great chocolate—sublime, a work of art, a sacred substance of ritual importance in Mesoamerican antiquity—deserved my undivided attention. I was not particularly predisposed to pairing my chocolate with anything. If the goddess of cacao was a jealous deity like the one in the Hebrew Scriptures, why would anyone risk abusing her chocolatey essence with an alcoholic beverage? Or heaven forbid—something as pungent as cheese!

The pleasure of chocolate's glorious flavors was not the entire story for me; it was also a gateway to achieving a similar deep focus to the one I had long ago experienced in meditation. Discovering that commonality had inspired me to try chocolate as a way to introduce people to the basics of meditation. Later, as the director of an Interfaith congregation, I went on to use it ritually. Instead of wine or bread used in Old World traditions, we blessed New World cacao and shared it. It proved disarming, welcoming and inclusive, without carrying any off-putting denominational baggage for people turned off by mainstream religions. If you'd like to know more about how I incorporated cacao and chocolate into spiritual and ritual practice, you may enjoy the first book in this Deep Tasting series where I told the story of my parallel journeys in chocolate and spirituality. The point is, for me, chocolate deserved veneration.

And as a reviewer, chocolate demanded serious study, dedication and discipline. I took my chocolate in the morning, instead of coffee, on a virgin palate, untainted by the influence of any other aromas or flavors. "Chocolate," I often declared to startled participants at social gatherings, "is an appetizer, not a dessert!" Having a meal beforehand, I would explain, influenced the perception of the smell and taste of the chocolate. You would be correct to call me a purist, in a sense. But you'd be in error to think me puritanical. A bit of indulgence– all good. I get the chocolate cake thing, the chocolate ice cream, the chocolate-whatever dessert. And as dessert, what is essential, is a rich, naked cocoa-flavored experience. It's enjoyable. It's fun. It's delicious, sure! But that's not the same as a deeply focused tasting. It is merely pleasurable. It comes, it goes, and it can leave craving and longing in its wake. But deep tasting, savoring profoundly, that is something else entirely. So what could prompt me to pivot somewhat in my viewpoint? Hell, what motivated me to "chill," to lighten up?

I'd been watching others in the chocolate world conduct pairing sessions: chocolate with wine, chocolate with beer, chocolate with cheese, chocolate with your Uncle Ned... But I hadn't seen much pairing with whiskey or whisky, even though bourbon and other whiskeys had been used to flavor creamy bonbon centers (*ganache*) and, more recently, bars of chocolate. What no one had been talking much about was pairing bars with drams of whiskey. Perhaps, because you need extensive experience as a taster of both items to do a credible job of mating the two. Knowledge takes a lot of time and effort to acquire. You need to understand the lexicon of those substances, appreciate how it was made, be familiar with their history and culture, but above all, be intimate with the respective aromas and flavors of chocolate and whiskey. If you can't speak the flavor language of master distillers and chocolate makers, you won't avoid the pitfalls, the clashes and downright incompatibilities. Your search to make the perfect match will be haphazard, hit or miss. It's potentially embarrassing. And it's certainly a waste of time.

Distillers are not suddenly hatched. Master whiskey distillers are years in the making. And people do not become fine chocolate experts over-night either. So why did people seem so cavalier playing this pairing game? I suspect it's largely for financial reasons. Liquor is more expensive than chocolate. You can ask a higher price for events featuring them paired. Chocolate is sexy. Whiskey is sexy. Why not put them together? Sexy, sexy, sexy. Palate porno. Those who do not fully experience chocolate or whiskey can easily succumb to the credo of consumers: if chocolate is good, and wine, beer or whiskey are good, then surely good plus good must equal delicious. Well, no. Not that simple. The resulting pair can be a subtractive experience rather than additive, even when we love the individuals. And sometimes, pairing is simply beside the point; for example, when a chocolate or whiskey is so sublime, that you don't want any additional aromas or flavors to interfere with sensory impressions.

However, armed with the bona fides of a taster, I decided I could no longer stand on the sidelines. I had the training in the social sciences to undertake this effort in a systematic way. A perennial student, I began reading the classics on scotch and bourbon. I discovered, that like wine and chocolate, researchers had developed flavor profiles of whisky and bourbon and rye. It dawned on me that I might be able to develop a method to aid people who, for whatever reason, wanted to wed sacred chocolate with noble spirit. By contributing to confidence in your palate, this book might enable you to withstand hype when confronted with it. You could purchase great chocolate and whiskey without having your pockets picked. And hopefully, my years as a meditator will enable me to help readers find a "middle way"—not of denial or overindulgence, but a mindful, moderate and responsible way of enjoying the gifts of both chocolate and whiskey.

2

CRAFT DISTILLERS AND CRAFT CHOCOLATE MAKERS

People get into the industry thinking they're going to make a big killing—that they're going to be the next Grey Goose. And they don't realize how long it takes to do all of this and how much money is involved...
— Ralph Erenzo,
founder, Tuthilltown Spirits

NOT EVERY WHISKEY IN THIS BOOK was created by a "craft" distillery. But most of the chocolates were made by craft, or artisan, chocolate makers. What is a craft distiller? And what is a craft chocolate maker?

According to a press release issued October 18, 2016 by the American Craft Spirits Association, there are more than 1,315 identified craft spirit producers in the USA. A craft spirit distiller is defined by the ACSA as one that produces fewer than 750,000 proof gallons (315, 451 9-liter cases) annually. Whisky Advocate magazine cites these same numbers in their recent issue and projects the current rate of growth could result in over 2,800 distillers by 2020. There are over 104 in my home state of New York alone! Just for the sake of comparison, according to the Scottish Whisky Association, there are only 115 distilleries licensed to produce scotch in Scotland. By the way, the country that consumes the most scotch... France! Really.

The market share of craft spirit is just 2.2 percent of the total amount of spirit consumed in the USA. There is enormous potential for growth, provided the craft distillers can make the case for their unique products to retailers, with their already overstocked shelves, as well as to consumers. The craft spirit stories will have to be compelling enough to justify, in many cases, a pricy differential, and to compete with the more predictable quality of the well-established spirits. Through a variety of means, from free tastings at local liquor stores to whiskey festivals, many craft distillers are breaking through and finding consumers. But most craft distillers will find distribution challenging.

Some craft brands, such as, Louisville Distilling Company's Angel's Envy and Tuthilltown's Hudson, and recently, Westland Distillery of Seattle, have been successful enough to be snapped up by international spirit conglomerates, such as Bacardi, William Grant & Sons and Rémy Cointreau, respectively. These international spirit mega-companies claim a diverse range of spirits under their umbrellas through acquisitions. They own controlling shares—or entire companies outright—and can efficiently distribute vodka, gin, rum, whiskey and other spirits.

But craft distilling operations exist not just as external acquisitions. Traditional distilling companies have not been sleeping through the craft movement. Some large companies have launched their own craft lines in-house, from Sazerac with Buffalo Trace's Eagle Rare to Beam Suntory with Jim Beam's Basil Hayden and Bookers. In the USA, Scotland, and around the world, the mergers and acquisitions of distilleries have proceeded at a dizzying pace in the last few decades. While there are fewer well-established independents left standing, legally and financially, the best subsidiaries seem to be operating with enough autonomy to survive and thrive as distinct brands. At least from the outside, the spirit conglomerates seem to be doing a better job of encouraging experimentation and integrity of the brand than in the chocolate world.

Most of us in the chocolate world attribute the beginning of the craft or artisan chocolate movement in the USA with the establishment of Scharffen Berger Chocolate Maker, by Robert Steinberg and John Scharffenberger in the mid 1990s, following on the heels of the craft wine movement. In fact, John Scharffenberger himself participated in the latter before partnering with Robert Steinberg. The craft whiskey movement also began in the 90s. Artisan beer and ale brewing predate both the wine and chocolate artisan waves by about a decade. That craft beer movement was a predecessor is significant because the making of grain into beer is a step before distilling; indeed, some early craft brewers later went on to distill.

An artisan, or craft, chocolate maker is assumed to produce far less chocolate than industrial chocolate manufacturers. But how much? There is currently no annual output stated as a prerequisite of membership in any organization comparable to the American Craft Spirits Association. There was one—The Craft Chocolate Makers of America (CCMA)—but it is no longer in existence. However, we in the chocolate world may be on our way to creating consensus that began with early attempts by the now-defunct CCMA. Recently, The Fine Cacao and Chocolate

Institute's (FCCI) Executive Director, Dr. Carla D. Martin published in that organization's blog that a small craft or "specialty" chocolate maker might produce 200 metric tons or less per year. That seems generously inclusive to me. Most small craft chocolate makers don't produce anywhere near that. How many actually do produce in the neighborhood of 200 metric tons? I can only think of a possible few. If we assume that most chocolate bars weigh between 1.76 and 3.5 ounces, that comes to somewhere between 2,015,657 to 4,008,409 bars per year. But the 200-metric ton figure is an upper limit. Anyone producing more than 200 metric tons would be considered a "specialty chocolate manufacturer," meaning that they produce industrial-size quantities but use fine flavor, versus bulk commodity, cacao beans. Defining craft chocolate makers by the size of their production is still a work in progress. Let's look at a description of what they actually do.

The artisan chocolate maker, as defined by the Fine Chocolate Industry Association (FCIA), is assumed to be involved in the making of the product every step of the way, from bean to the finished bar. In America, at least, the term "chocolate maker" is distinguished from "chocolatier," who may use the chocolate maker's or chocolate manufacturer's product to create their own bars, bonbons, or other chocolate-based confections. In my experience, Europeans may not make a distinction between the two, calling both chocolatiers.

Whether chocolate maker or chocolatier, the chocolate community expects transparency in terms of packaging and advertising. If someone claims to be producing chocolate "bean to bar," they better be doing so, or all hell will break loose if found out. There seem to be fewer scandals in the whiskey world and less transparency. There are companies that call themselves craft spirit producers that are merely bottlers. Some may age or finish the spirit before bottling it under their own labels, yet fail to disclose the source of the original, distilled spirit. There is a minimal aging of two years that must take place before you can sell anything as a straight whiskey in America. That's a lot of time with no money coming in. Therefore, upstarts may take a short cut until they have mature whiskey to bottle. Nothing wrong with that, unless they're not being transparent about it.

While researching this book, I encountered whiskey company "ambassadors" (representatives) at tastings. Because I wanted to feature actual distillers in this book, I would ask the reps pointedly about it. Most were honest with me. But I learned to read bottles with caution and to not be timid about contacting companies for more information. For starters, look for the words "distilled by" versus "bottled by." Use of the term "distillery" doesn't mean they actually distilled that particular spirit; it just means they distill something on premises.

Compared to craft distillers, there are far fewer craft chocolate makers in the USA. Before ceasing operation, the Craft Chocolate Makers of America had documented about 112 in 2014, but that number continues to soar. Pashmina Lalchandani at the Bar and Cocoa blog (blog.barandcocoa.com) included approximately 175 entries in the United States recently, but those numbers may have changed. The survey, according to the website's owner, Pashmina Lalchandani, was conducted initially through internet search alone, but recently she opened her database to contributors in the chocolate community, worldwide. I turned to the website of the Fine Chocolate Industry Association to get some answers, but their count seems to reflect only members. If so, that can mean a lot of businesses unaccounted for. Dr. Martin, in her recent FCCI blog article reported that out of 481 specialty chocolate makers and manufacturers, globally, approximately 450 fell into the smaller business category of specialty chocolate maker (craft chocolate maker). In the USA, she counted 192 specialty chocolate makers and manufacturers. Assuming that a small number of those 192 fall into the larger manufacturing category, we have to figure that somewhat less than 192, but, probably, more than 175 may be said to fall into the craft chocolate maker category. A ball park figure will have to do for now. The count is still an emerging story, and, to some extent, always will be, as businesses close and others open. But as you can see, the craft chocolate movement is dwarfed by the ranks of craft distillers.

A new chocolate maker seems to pop up every day. And you might be tempted to conclude that there is still plenty of room for more chocolate makers, compared to the craft spirit makers. However, unlike liquor, there are fewer stores that just sell chocolate bars. That means competing for shelf space in gourmet food shops, health food stores, mixed-use brick and mortar stores; distributing through online retailers; and/ or selling your product on your own website. However, it's possible both industries are reaching something of a saturation point, at least in the United States. For many mature craft distillers, distribution without large, corporate partnership is limited. Many have felt compelled to sell controlling shares, if not the entire company out-right, to the liquor conglomerates in order to reach more consumers. To succeed going forward, however, newcomers in both worlds who wish to remain independent will increasingly need to carve out regional and specialty followings. The unspoken question is how big you want your company to grow.

3

BLENDS VERSUS SINGLE ORIGINS AND SINGLE MALTS

Every category has its snobs: music, books, movies. There are so many things a man is only pressured into liking or disliking.
— *Criss Jami*

CHOCOLATE

I'LL NEVER FORGET MY FIRST tasting of Scharffen Berger chocolate in the mid- 90s. A typical American girl, I was brought up on Hershey and Mars bars, and, later, Cadbury, while living in London. In the 80s, I found sanctuary in the bittersweet flavors of imported Lindt. That dark prince of chocolate, so roasted, so earthy, so bitter-sweet, kissed my drowsy mouth. Something inside me awakened as he faded away, trailing his mystery. Was he real? Was he an illusion? It didn't matter. I wasn't searching for more, and I remained faithful to the prince for quite a while. Then, along came Scharffen Berger. A complex and wondrous encounter. So satisfying for so long, then, too...so long! So many suitors in the guise of artisan chocolates.

The late American physician Robert Steinberg had a dream. He had traveled widely and known European chocolate. Why wasn't this kind of chocolate being produced in the United States? Determined to try his hand at it, he went to Lyon, France to learn chocolate making at Bernachon. Entrepreneur John Scharffenberger knew Robert while he was still practicing medicine. John had successfully produced and marketed wine, and joined with Robert to start an artisanal chocolate company. When their company, Scharffen Berger Chocolate Maker, released their first offering, it was in the form of baking bars for the culinary industry. They bought the finest cacao beans from a variety of regions to create a blended chocolate bar. Robert's sister, Nancy, and I had been friends, and still are, so I was privileged to taste Scharffen Berger's first efforts before commercial release. At that time, it was packed with the flavors of rich fruit and subtly roasted notes of coffee and cocoa and traces of nuts. The fruit profile was bold, and this brightness would come to influence the next waves of American artisan chocolate makers. But Scharffen Berger has changed since Hershey bought the company in 2005. While the flavor declined after several years under Hershey, the blended bars would remain relatively stable for a few years at a time. But the quality now is far from what it was. To my taste buds, the flavor profile of their signature bar has completely changed. Given my history with the brand, it is very sad for me.

Single origin chocolate bars, as opposed to blended bars, used to be defined as made from cacao beans from the same country, but it's more precise to define it as from a particular variety of cacao grown in a specific region, or even more precisely, grown by a regional group of farms, a farming cooperative, or at a large, single estate. Cacao beans change with every harvest, sometimes only subtly, sometimes dramatically. It all depends on climate, but also economic conditions, and even geopolitical events. A single origin bar is an adventure. And many of us like that taste of the unknown. Because Scharffen Berger was aimed at the culinary market, their first efforts were blended chocolates so it would be reproducible in recipes. SB could buy cacao beans from different regions even as harvests varied. They added the traditional vanilla to further increase flavor reliability, as do most of the European chocolate producers.

There are many wonderful chocolate companies in Europe making superb blended bars, from Italy's Amedei to France's Valrhona, and they use vanilla. It's classic. And some fine chocolate makers also use lecithin. This does not take away from their artistry or the pleasure of the experience. As long as they are transparent about listing the ingredients on the packaging, you know what you're getting. Their choice and yours. However, many in the craft chocolate movement use a minimum of ingredients, with many preferring just cacao and sugar. They want to show off the bean for what it can do. A small percentage may be purists or dogmatic, or even holier-than-thou snobs about it. But in my experience, most of those who insist on using just two ingredients are coming from a place of reverence. They want to optimize, not disguise, the beans' true nature—their intrinsic flavor properties. Therefore, they may not only refuse to add anything else to the recipe, they may also prefer to only lightly roast the beans. These "purists" respect cacao beans, and many carry that over to a respect for cacao's rain-forest home, the environment and the people and communities who grow and process cacao beans.

While still under the guidance of Robert and John, SB also produced small batches of single origin bars, some of which were absolutely stunning. We'd wait for them every year and rush to buy them before they sold out. It's been many years now since

SB, under the ownership of Big Chocolate Hershey, has created any excitement. Such a loss! Fortunately, the inspiration that Robert Steinberg and John Scharffenberger brought to American chocolate has survived corporate confinement; the artisan spirit has multiplied and reincarnated as a new generation of craft chocolate makers you will find listed in these pages. And not everyone is producing just single origin chocolate. Many craft chocolate makers who excel at that type are also producing blended bars. It's all about the flavor and the creative spirit. So there's lots of excitement to be had, whether you like single origin or blended chocolate, or like me, are delighted to try both.

The craft chocolate movement is world-wide now. You can get your excitement from as far as Australia, Fiji, Madagascar, Tanzania, the Philippines, and the Solomon Islands, as well as Latin America and the Caribbean. The United States is growing cacao and producing chocolate in Hawaii, and most recently again in Puerto Rico. I've even heard of some growing it in southern Florida, out of the 20 degree latitudinal zone on either side of the equator, long assumed as the narrow band where cacao can flourish. When it comes to cacao and chocolate, whether single origin or blend, rich flavor experiences await us.

WHISKY

Let's turn our attention to whisky. The biggest buzz word in reference to scotch for the last few decades has been single malt. But the largest selling scotch whiskies in the world are blends. In fact, blends constitute 90% of the scotch whisky market, with Johnny Walker the biggest seller. And there's a new generation of boutique blends with hefty price tags, such as Compass Box. Stick around long enough and everything comes back in style! But what's the difference between a single malt and a blend?

A single malt is a whisky distilled from malted barley, made by the same distillery. Now, here's where it gets a bit confusing. The single malt can be taken from different barrels, aged years apart, then "married" and "finished" in yet another cask before being bottled, and still be considered a single malt. It simply has to be made at the same distillery. So master distillers are actually master blenders using in-house whiskies. But don't use the word blend! Here's why. If even one drop from one distillery is mingled with a single malt from another, it must be labeled a blend. See why the word is verboten? A "blended scotch whisky," however, can, and usually does, contain another kind of grain whisky, unless the label reads, "blended malt scotch." A very pleasant, blended malt scotch is Monkey Shoulder, which combines the single malts from three different distilleries–Kininvie, Glendfiddich and Balvenie. Monkey Shoulder contains no other grain whiskies.

Master blenders may orchestrate dozens of single malts and grain whiskies to achieve the flavor profiles they seek. Small changes over the years may be lost on the average palate. As a result, if you order a Johnny Walker Black, you pretty well know what you're getting, whether in Hong Kong or Cape Town. Blends, originally invented by bottling merchants, not distillers, by the way, are recipes that can compensate for variations batch to batch and harvest to harvest. Blends were created to produce an overall pleasing effect, and most of all, since the early 20th century, they were designed to be used in cocktails and mixed drinks. And like the best blended chocolate, good blended scotch is also enjoyable straight on its own.

Whether in chocolate or whiskey, blending cacao beans or whiskeys produces a recognizable, similarly flavored product from harvest to harvest. The chef or the baker, the bartender, and, ultimately, the consumer, can anticipate a predictable taste result, whether for creating cookies and pastries or mixed drinks. And, by the way, you'll notice that I didn't talk about American bourbons and rye whiskeys or Canadian whiskies in relation to single-anything or blending–that's because the vast majority of North American whiskeys are in fact blended grains, and in the States this takes place before distillation. Let's be clear about this: Creating great chocolate or great whiskey blends is a work of art–the composing of aromatic, flavor and textural symphonies that are harmonious, balanced, delightful and memorable. Whether distillers or blenders, these are masters of their craft. Their senses, talents and experiences have pushed them to the top of their industries. If you should ever meet one of these masters, be humble in the presence of greatness.

The take-away: Blends are not lesser than single origins or single malts. You are not less discerning or ignorant if you prefer a blend. Don't be a single origin chocolate or single malt whisky snob. Run into an expert who isn't shy and enjoys putting the half-educated in their place, and they can make you look like a damned fool. The best chocolate, like the best whiskey, is the one that puts the biggest smile on your face. Period.

4

MODERATION AND MINDFULNESS

Moderation in all things, especially moderation.
— Ralph Waldo Emerson

MODERATION

I DOUBT ANY OTHER BOOK on whiskey or chocolate includes a chapter like this. It just isn't sexy enough to sell books. But I'm going to talk about the moderate consumption of chocolate and whiskey and what that truly means. And I'm going to discuss mindfulness as a way to achieve moderation. Ironically, it's also a way to fully experience pleasurable things. Mindfulness can be an indispensable life-skill. It comes to us from the East, from meditation, although, these days in the West it is popularly practiced in many healthcare and non- denominational settings. In other words, you do not need to take on another religion or another culture to practice this form of mindfulness. At the end of this chapter, there's a training exercise in nosing, that is, smelling the aromas of whiskey. The exercise utilizes mindfulness. So if you're tempted to skip this chapter, you will be rewarded for sticking around.

To be responsible in dispensing the information in this book, I need to be straight forward. As an Interfaith minister, I've encountered many people in 12-step programs, in recovery from substance abuse. They have my deepest respect for having the strength and courage to look their personal truth in the eye and turn their lives around. I'm not what people might think of as a "typical" minister, if by that they mean someone judgmental and self-righteous, or a paragon of virtue. I'm so far from that, it's not even funny. I guess you can figure that out by the fact that I would even write a book on pairing whiskey and chocolate. So I'm simply going to give you information and share some skills. It's up to you how to make use of them.

Moderation in this chapter isn't just about alcohol. As a consumer, I know that abuse of chocolate can also have health and interpersonal consequences. I have suffered from heart arrhythmias and weight issues, so I've personally had to consume both chocolate and whiskey at levels that are even less than amounts considered "moderate." That's no easy task for a reviewer or for a writer researching a book. I've had to do it, so I know it can be done. But most people don't have to limit themselves to the same degree. You probably don't. Yet for everyone, the issue of moderation is serious and needs to be understood. The enjoyment you seek in pairing chocolate and whiskey should be safe, as well as pleasurable.

Let's face this right on. Not everyone should drink whiskey, and not everyone should eat chocolate. If someone's diabetic or allergic to either chocolate or alcohol, they probably already know to proceed with caution. What if you must refrain from gluten? Here, you're on safe ground. Distillation removes the gluten proteins.

Other than cases requiring outright abstention, the reader is advised to consider their own health histories and risk factors when thinking about consuming chocolate or whiskey. A family history of alcoholism? Probably best to minimize the consumption of alcohol. Not sure of your risk? Consult a physician, if there's any question.

Just because there's a family history, doesn't mean you carry a dominant gene for diabetes or alcoholism. Want to know more? You might consider a referral for genetic testing and counseling. A lot of people are getting DNA testing these days for a host of reasons: from assessing disease risk to finding out their ethnic lineage. Make sure, if you get genetic testing, that the service provides a counselor who is certified by either the American Board of Medical Genetics (www.abmgg.org) or the American Board of Genetic Counseling (www.abgc.net) because the wrong interpretation of genetic testing can cause unnecessary anxiety, even tragedy. Make sure to get an accurate understanding of any test results.

Taking medications? Please ask your doctor or pharmacist to make sure there will be no harmful interactions if you consume alcohol. Prone to heart arrhythmias? The latest research suggests minimizing your alcohol intake, and that's long been the recommendation when it comes to the stimulants found in chocolate. A woman at risk for breast cancer is also advised to restrict alcohol. Restricting or limiting does not mean you have to deny yourself an occasional pleasurable sip. Again, know your risks!

What is moderate drinking? Guidelines suggest no more than one drink for a woman, and two for a man, per day. A single drink is defined as 1.5 ounces (44.36 ml) of spirits that are 80 proof, 5 ounces (147.87 ml) of wine, and 12 ounces (354.88 ml) of beer. If the whiskey is 90 proof or more, adjust the serving size downward. However, while that is considered moderate drinking, we may want to rethink the per day part in the definition.

It's long been known that excessive drinking can contribute to dementia, among other serious health problems. However, even moderate daily consumption has been shown to relate to demonstrable shrinking of the brain with accompanying declines in cognition and learning. But what about the heart? For overall heart health, a small amount of alcohol was thought, until recently, to be beneficial. But the latest information in the Harvard Health Letter (August 2017) now throws cold water on these alleged benefits. There are reasons to doubt some of the earlier studies. Personally, I always want to know who is funding the research. When I hear any beverage or food group is behind it, I'm suspicious. So don't drink because you think it may be good for the heart. Not yet. Stay tuned for future studies. Meanwhile, there are other things to do to keep your heart healthy—like exercise!

There have been a number of studies touting the health benefits of dark chocolate on blood pressure, the heart and the aging brain. But those benefits will be undone by overindulgence that leads to obesity. Again, moderation is key. What is a moderate serving of dark chocolate? I don't advise going by the average serving listed on the nutritional information on chocolate packaging. An extra 200 calories a day can really pack on the weight for many of us. Consider your personal daily caloric intake target and activity level, for starters. Some studies suggest that 200 grams of dark chocolate a week can be good for your health. That's 28.57 grams (1 ounce), per day. Many chocolate bars weigh 85 grams or approximately 3 ounces. That's closer to 3 servings per day in that bar, not the 2 most cite on the labels. Sorry! These manufacturers are making many of us fat.

That's the physical side of the story. What about the

psychological? We need to be honest with ourselves. What are our emotional vulnerabilities? How do we manage stress in our lives? Any food or drink, but particularly chocolate and alcohol, can be used to self-medicate. "Oh, I need it for energy." "I need it to relax." "I need to reward myself." " I deserve a break." "I'm just going through a rough patch." These are rationalizations. "I can handle one more." "I don't need anyone to tell me how much to drink." "What do you mean, don't I think I've eaten enough chocolate?" These are denials. How often might you, or someone you know, be engaging in rationalization or denial by saying or thinking these things? Once a week? More than a few times a week? Daily? By the way, the most popular addictive self-medicating drug in the USA? Not opiates, serious as they are. Coffee! Go cold turkey and watch yourself experience withdrawal symptoms: headaches, the blahs, mood swings. Listen to yourself deny your addiction and rationalize the need to get a caffeine-fix.

Alcohol and chocolate both have histories of being used for medicinal reasons. While most of the original medical reasons for prescribing them are now considered obsolete by modern medicine, there are times in cases of acute psychological shock or grief–an acute, one-time situation–where whiskey might be helpful. But more than once is getting into self-medicating territory. The long- term patterns of self-medicating can have dire consequences on health and relationships. Need to medicate? Seek medical intervention. Neither whiskey nor chocolate is appropriate for handling on-going stress or depression. But meditation is! Counseling is! Peer support is!

So, are you capable of consuming chocolate or whiskey with moderation? Here's a test. Can you, or someone you may be concerned about, eat just 1-2 squares of chocolate and walk away? Can you have one shot of whiskey and walk away? Or do you find it difficult to refuse a second helping of chocolate or whiskey? If so, that's a red flag. Here is where responsible decision-making needs to kick in.

If, by the end of this book, you cannot enjoy just 1-2 squares of chocolate or a standard serving of whiskey, then that's a signal that your physical constitution may not be able to tolerate chocolate or whiskey. Walk away. Personally, I have trouble eating just a small portion of potato chips. So I have to stay away from them, unless I make a very strong effort to eat them mindfully. Even so, the effort is usually not worth it. It complicates my life far less to just stay away from them. Want to torture me? Feed me one potato chip, tantalize me by waving the rest of the bag in my face– and you could probably get away with every password I've ever keystroked.

So, what's your weakness? Are you a chocophile or a chocoholic? Are you a whiskey lover or an alcoholic? There's a wide world to enjoy out there that doesn't necessarily require indulgence in a substance that controls you, rather than the other way around. Whether chocolate or alcohol... or potato chips. Respect your own body and mind. It doesn't make you less of a person if you can't tolerate a particular substance. It makes you more of a person, a master of your own destiny, if you can honestly recognize and respect your own constitution and live a life of integrity.

We all have vulnerabilities. It turns out that anything pleasurable produces endorphins that our neural receptors crave. The desire to produce these feel-good chemicals can become addictive. Some substances can trigger us more easily than others. It's individual and a matter of degree. For some substances it's all or nothing—like my potato chips. The substances that are just mild or moderate triggers are those we can best work with using mindfulness, behavioral therapy and old fashioned "self-control."

Most of us need skills to manage the pleasurable consumption of that which can easily become a habit. It need not be just food or drink. Psychologists have recognized that even technology can be addictive. People seem to be addicted to social media and to texting. Studies have shown that when people suddenly stop these activities, they show increased stress and anxiety, classic signs related to addiction. The social media and texting addict brain cells crave the engagement. When I see people pushing baby carriages into traffic as they cross the street because they can't stop texting, I say to myself, there's a device that person needs to let go of.

These days, you will often see whiskey makers publish "drink responsibly," in advertisements and on their websites. I would add, "consume chocolate and whiskey mindfully," as well. The spirits industry has made serious commitments to education about moderation in alcohol consumption. The Distilled Spirits Council of the United States (discus.org) and the Scotch Whisky Association (scotch- whisky.org.uk) in the United Kingdom both promote responsible drinking on their websites to combat drunk driving and underage drinking, as well as to educate the public on other topics related to how to drink moderately. You've probably heard people say that they aren't going to drink the "hard" stuff, just have a beer or a glass of wine to avoid drinking too much. Both DISCUS and the SWA say that there is no such thing as a "moderate" alcoholic beverage type. A shot of whiskey is comparable in alcohol content to a glass of beer or a glass of wine. In other words, a standard serving is comparable across beverage types. DISCUS has created the Foundation for Advancing Alcohol Responsibility. For more information, visit their website: responsibility.org. At the end of this book, you will find the Resources section in case you know anyone who is struggling with over-consumption of whiskey or chocolate.

MINDFULNESS

How can you be sure that you are able to indulge with moderation without slipping into overindulgence? It can be tricky. Let me introduce you to a form of applied meditation—mindfulness—that can help. In short, moderation achieved through mindfulness can be seen as the practice of letting go of craving by considering it a form of intrusion. The intrusion can take the form of thoughts or sensations. For example, when you're trying to work and you get a thought like: "That chocolate I had earlier was so good. I've got to have more. Now!" or "I feel stressed. I know chocolate will make me feel better." Both cases illustrate distracting thoughts or sensations. The solution is something else upon which to focus. We'll get to that in a moment. Because it also happens that while you are attempting to enjoy chocolate or whiskey, thoughts and sensations can intrude upon that experience, as well. For example, while trying to focus on flavor, out of nowhere, you find yourself thinking things that are totally irrelevant to the experience of tasting whiskey or chocolate. Here's an experiment: try to very slowly drink your next cup of coffee or tea, and see how many thoughts or sensations intrude. Probably one every few seconds. See if you can catch your mind in the act of creating a distraction, when all you want to do is just focus on the deep, rich flavor of that cup of coffee (or tea).

This is how mindfulness meditation basically works: focus, recognize any distractions, let go of them by refocusing. With both chocolate and whiskey, the touchstone upon which to focus and refocus is the unfolding of aromas, flavors and textures. The intruding or distracting thought or sensation may be anything, such as "Gee, I forgot to call back my friend, George," or "Why is my back feeling itchy?" or "What did Jim mean yesterday by that stupid remark?" or "My neck feels tight, why is it tight, what did I do, oh, right, I was at the gym…" or "I need to check my email."

Some of these intrusive thoughts take on a life of their own and transport us mentally so far away from what we're doing, we can forget what time it is or where we are for a few moments. You might be trying to taste chocolate or whiskey. And instead of enjoying them, these thoughts and sensations steal the experience away from you by taking up your time, attention and energy. Ironically, the mental processes that cheat us of fully experiencing pleasure are the same ones that enable craving (which is just a thought or sensation, after all) to rob us of our equanimity.

The necessary skill underlying the moderating of pleasure is a technique that combines highly focused, profound savoring while tuning out or letting go of distracting thoughts or sensations. I call this form of mindfulness, as specifically applied to food or drink "deep tasting." Less is more when we fully savor and fully experience. Like any skill, practice is required. So, whether tasting chocolate or whiskey, you will be focusing, recognizing distractions, then letting go of them by immediately refocusing. When we do that, we can enjoy the present morsel, the present sip, the present moment. When we fully appreciate, we can feel complete when that discrete experience has ended. Enough is enough, even when the experience has been delicious. The experience ends. It's over. Time to get on with something else.

If we begin to crave more of the item we just enjoyed, we can then use the same skill that we applied while tasting to tune out any longing for more. How very convenient! By redirecting ourselves from the annoying voice of desire, we interrupt the excitation of our neural receptors. Give those receptors a rest! Keep redirecting your attention, perhaps just to simple breathing– inhale, exhale– observe your respirations without effort. Or you can redirect your attention to an action, such as walking, step after step, feel yourself moving, feel your muscles working. Suddenly the craving has gone, and you don't even notice that it left you. By interrupting the loop of tasting and craving, we stop stimulating those pleasure-demanding receptor cells and avoid habit formation. Twelve-step programs are famous for saying "One day at a time." I say, when dealing with craving, it's "One moment at a time."

Dealing successfully with these receptor cells is like handling a greedy creature. You give them a sip, you give them a morsel, you enjoy it. Then you want to get on with something else. But the cells don't want to let go of you. "More, give me more!" they chatter at you like a tree full of insane parrots. Craving will make you feel vaguely or hugely uncomfortable until you give in. But guess what, a few minutes after giving in, after completing the next sip or the next morsel, they're back at it–"Give me more. Just one more sip. I promise. Just one more piece of chocolate."

Endorphin receptors are liars! And they need to be called out. Cut them off. They'll never be satisfied. So decide exactly how much you want to consume in advance, and stick to it. You be the boss. If craving rears its ugly head, tell it, you're wise to it. Just as you will learn to focus on aromas and flavors and let go of any distractions, you can learn to treat craving those very same substances as a distraction when you haven't planned to enjoy it at that particular time. Take a breath and just let the craving go. Turn your mind away by focusing on something else, or just on your breathing for a few minutes. Practice walking away by, well– walking away! And repeat that turning away as often as necessary. It may take hours or days of turning away or refocusing. When to stop? When you are the one deciding when to indulge, and you're not taking orders from the craving monster.

With the mindful-savoring skill, introduced in book one of the Deep Tasting series, *Deep Tasting: A Chocolate Lover's*

Guide To Meditation, and reintroduced here, you can learn how to indulge, without overindulging. You can include chocolate, or spirits, or anything else on a diet and actually lose weight. You might want to check out Chapter Eight in *Deep Tasting: A Chocolate Lover's Guide To Meditation*–it's about how to eat chocolate and lose weight! We can also do this with alcohol.

When we fail to apply the mindfulness practice of *Deep Tasting*, when we are distracted by anything, a thought, a physical sensation, a noise, or someone walking by, we miss flavors as they unfold. We haven't maximized the intense pleasure of the moment. By the time we've redirected our attention back to the taste, another flavor has emerged and disappeared. We are in danger of missing the experience. If we're quick to notice that we've been distracted, we might catch up to the next flavor to appear. The need to pivot from distractions and stay focused is very clear in the case of chocolate–because it melts!–which is why I found it such a unique tool for introducing people to meditation. You'll get a chance to sample this technique, generically applied to chocolate, in the chapter "How To Taste." You can get more specific versions of the meditation technique in my first book and by listening to the audio recordings of guided tastings on my website. But what about whiskey? It doesn't melt. Is it still something to which we can consider a touch-stone for attention? Well, yes, within each sip flavors arise, then fade away. Whiskey too changes moment by moment and into the finish. Divert your attention for a second and you will miss a flavor or texture. But we can learn some fundamentals of deep tasting mindfulness, even before tasting the whiskey.

We can start with aroma. When I go to whiskey tastings, I go armed; that is, I take along a few items: a stainless steel flask, in case I want to take a sample home, a bottle of spring water to cleanse my palate between tastings, and a small glass bottle of distilled or spring water with an eye-dropper. (The reason I don't use tap water is that fluoride or chlorine can change the flavor.) I've been pleasantly surprised by slipping a drop of spring water into an otherwise "unimpressive" spirit. If you were to introduce a droplet of water, you'd see how that it can often open up the aroma and flavor further, revealing new notes, deemphasizing some or emphasizing others. While all the chocolate bar and whiskey pairings in this book were conducted by tasting the spirit straight up or neat (nothing added), I encourage you to go beyond this book. Try the whiskey neat with the chocolate, first. Later if you like the whiskey, try it with a drop of water. Whatever you enjoy. Take what you learn here, then experiment.

Let's start with the training exercise in the text box entitled: Nosing (Smelling) with Mindfulness.

nosing (smelling) with mindfulness

This is a training exercise. The objective is to help you focus on aromas. It should take you between 10 and 15 minutes. We will be adding water for this exercise, but that is entirely optional as you go about tasting the recommended pairings later in this book.

Set up
You will need a Glencairn-type glass (pictured on the cover of this book) or a small brandy snifter, or a small, tulip-shaped wine glass will also work. I wouldn't use a champagne glass, however. The main idea is that the glass should have a somewhat broad bottom and narrower neck that directs the aromas upward without dispersing them.
Use any type of whisky, or whiskey, you may have on hand, or purchase one recommended in the chapter "Let's Go Shopping!" You will also need a water bottle with a small opening over the cap, or a bottle with an eyedropper. Place distilled or spring water in the bottle.
Pour approximately 1 ounce (30 ml) of whiskey into the glass.

Prepare
Turn off the ringer on your phone. Sit comfortably and free of any distractions. Make sure there are no competing odors (hand soap or lotion or any environmental odors). Make sure you will not be disturbed by anyone for about 15 minutes.

We're going to witness how whiskey aroma changes as it breathes, then how it may be altered with water. You will practice focusing while making mental note of any aromatic changes as you nose it intermittently. No need to recall impressions at this time. Just experience them and let them go. Keep your mouth slightly open as you inhale.

As you go about nosing, if you are distracted by any thoughts or sensations, immediately refocus on the aroma, or count to ten, then sniff again.

Ready to begin?
Take a quick, first sniff, but not too close to the rim. You will experience the volatility of the alcohol. If you get too close for too long, it will burn—avoid that.

Wait approximately five minutes. Count to ten. Take another quick sniff. Any decrease in the alcohol vapors?

If you are distracted by any thought or sensation, remember to immediately refocus on counting (to clear your nose, as well as refocus), then sniff again.

nosing (smelling) with mindfulness

Count to ten. Pick up the glass and turn it up, almost horizontally toward your nose. With your nose just above the top rim, take a quick whiff, then pull away. What aromas do you detect? Anything floral or fruity? Count to ten, try it again. What did you smell this time?

Count to ten. Place your nose toward the upper middle of the glass opening. Take a slightly longer whiff, then pull away. Can you detect changes in aroma? Can you detect anything winey or grainy or malty?

Count to ten. Lower your nose, pointing it toward the bottom rim. Take a more leisurely whiff. Any spicy or woody aromas? Any smoky or earthy aromas?

Next, put one tiny drop of water into the whiskey. Gently, give the glass a semi-swirl. Count to ten, then take another whiff. If your mind wanders, refocus right away and smell it again. Sniff toward the top rim. What aromas appear now?

Count to ten, take a sniff—toward the middle, then the bottom rim. What aromas do you detect now?

Add another drop of water. Count to ten. Sniff again at all three levels of the glass. Observe any changes in the aroma.

Repeat until the aroma seems to stabilize.

5

LET'S GO SHOPPING!

Always carry a flagon of whiskey in case of snakebite, and, furthermore, always carry a small snake.
– W. C. Fields

If she was going to die, she wanted to go out with chocolate in one hand and a shopping bag in the other.
— Caroline Hanson

HERE'S WHAT WE'LL ACCOMPLISH in this chapter:
1.   Understand what we'll be shopping for and why.
2.   Make a shopping list for low cost, easy-to-find chocolate bars and whiskeys.
3.   Buy the easy-to-find chocolates for tasting exercises.
4.   Buy the easy-to-find whiskeys for tasting exercises.

A FEW ESSENTIAL NOTES BEFORE WE GO SHOPPING

We're going to take a short break now to make a shopping list, then go look for the chocolate bars and whiskeys we will be using in the next chapter. Even if you already have a bar of one of the fine chocolates or whiskeys listed later in this book, please stop here and make a note of the ones in the present chapter. *The list in this chapter does not imply a statement of quality, endorsement, or preference.* These chocolates and whiskeys are represented simply as easy-to-find tools to explore your taste preferences and to acquire some basic tasting skills. So, consult the lists below, go to your local gourmet supermarket or health food store for the chocolate bars, and to a well-stocked liquor store for the whiskeys

We're going to start with chocolates that are widely distributed, most easily obtainable, and relatively inexpensive. Depending on where you live, you may not find all of them in your immediate area, of course. You don't have to. Just try to find ones suggested for pairing with the whiskeys listed with the asterisks (*) in front of them. These are brands recognized around the world. Whenever possible, I've tried to give you alternatives, marked with "s" for substitute. The chocolate companies are distributed in North America, Europe and some parts of the Caribbean and South America. The bars are made in France, Ecuador, Madagascar, the United Kingdom, the United States and the Caribbean, of cacao beans from a variety of regions. They contain varying arrays of aromatic and flavor notes called "flavor profiles." If you don't live in a major city, there are always the online stores. While I try to use brands that ethically source their chocolate-making materials, promote ecologic and economic sustainability, and economic justice, you may wish to visit the company websites to see if their practices are consistent with your own standards..

We're going to shop for widely-distributed, affordable whiskeys that represent varying styles: from peated, smoky scotch to fruity or sherried scotch, North American high corn content bourbon, high

whiskey lingo

PEAT

A couple of things to know with regard to scotch and other peated whiskies.

Peat refers to layers of soil formed by plants and minerals that have built up over millennia and have been traditionally dug up from deep peat bogs, then fed into the fireplaces or furnaces for fuel. In terms of whisky, after barley has been soaked and partially germinated, it must be dried. Peat is the fuel used in a kiln to dry this malted barley, the basic grain used to make single malt scotch. The peat imparts smoke and aromas of the burning plants and minerals– whether they be of the sea from the Hebrides or heather from the Highlands, whatever had become embedded in the soil over the eons.

TERROIR AND FLAVOR

Regional characteristics of the peat, along with the water and grain, the air and the particular warehousing practices contribute to what is called terroir. But there are two other factors that contribute to the final aromatic and flavor profiles. The first is the kind of still, or stills, used for distillation. The type of metal, shape and length, and how many times the liquid is distilled produce varying characteristics. Whiskey can be distilled any number of times the whiskey maker desires. Ireland, for example, is famous for triple distilling. Second, it is estimated that up to 60-80 % of the final profile of the whiskey comes from the maturation process—the type and condition of the wood used in the barrels and casks during initial aging, and the "finishing" process. During aging in the warehouse, the environment plays a role—the heat, the humidity, the air itself. These also figure into terroir.

WOOD AND AGING

Any whiskey, once it has been distilled, is placed into some kind of oak barrel. It can be European oak, French oak, Japanese oak, Canadian oak, or most commonly, these days, American white oak. Scottish distilleries used to use emptied—or "ex"—sherry barrels, or a variety of plain, toasted, European oak barrels. However, the consumption of sherry has sharply declined in Great Britain since the early 20th century. That means

whiskey lingo

fewer ex-sherry casks. Now they have to be specially imported for a single purpose, and that is added expense. Fortunately, American bourbon distilleries have to sell off used bourbon barrels. In the United States, some clever coopers–the barrel makers– with Prohibition and the Great Depression still a desperate memory, lobbied to have laws created, stipulating that whiskey must be aged in brand-new, charred barrels.

What to do with the empty, used barrels then? Sell them to the Brits! Well, not just to the UK, a lot of countries now use ex-bourbon barrels. When someone talks about traditional scotch whisky, you might wonder how far back they are referring, because the flavor of scotch whisky has changed over the last century due to the use of American ex-bourbon barrels. And we are probably, right now, at the inflection point for the most intense flavor changes in the world of whiskey. World-wide, distilleries are experimenting with aging and finishing in a variety of ex-barrels. In the United States, some craft whiskeys are being finished in ex-sherry, ex-port, various types of ex-wine, and ex-rum casks. The same is occurring in Britain and across the globe. With bourbon barrels going eastward and sherry casks going westward, the process has gone full circle. We'll talk more about aging and finishing in Chapter 7.

FINISHING

After the initial aging process, the whiskey may be placed in other barrels or casks that have held another type of liquor–bourbon, sherry or port, most commonly, but also various wines, cognac, and rum–and remain in those containers to soak up the residual flavors left in the wood. The period of time spent finishing is usually less than the initial aging period–generally, just six months to a year–but there's no duration requirement. During finishing, all the whiskeys that will be bottled in one release or expression are brought together and "married" in the same cask. Sometimes this marriage is quite polygamous!

wheat content bourbon, and high rye content bourbon and rye whiskey.

We're going to find out which, if any, types of whiskeys and chocolates you may prefer, and which whiskeys, when paired with which chocolates, are complementary. Later in this book, I will present some results of analyzed data that predict chocolate and whiskey duos that are compatible, and which ones are actually an additive experience. For example, whereas complementary is 1+1=2, my goal was to find pairs that were 1+1=3; in other words, ones that created an experience that brought out new flavor characteristics not necessarily evident in either the whiskey or the chocolate on their own.

People in the whiskey world have been studying the flavor profiles of scotch, bourbon and rye for many years, just as we have been doing in the chocolate world. Distilleries and industrial chocolate manufacturers have had a vested interest and the resources, along with allied industry associations, to conduct this research, but there are scholars and writers who also deserve special recognition. And you will find these contributors cited in Chapter 8, where you will learn more about flavor and flavor profiles, as well as a vocabulary of descriptors to use for various types of chocolates and whiskeys.

But for now, we can think simply, and broadly, about scotch types as existing along a continuum from peaty/smoky to fruity/sherried (as shown on the horizontal axis of Table 1)

TABLE 1
SCOTCH SINGLE MALTS (BARLEY-BASED)

PEATED....SMOKY

FULL-BODIED, RICH, WOOD, SPICY

LIGHT-BODIED, DELICATE, SWEET, CREAMY, FLORAL

FRUITY....SHERRIED

As can be seen in *Table 1*, a continuum is represented along the horizontal line that reflects whether the aromatics and flavor of the scotch are more heavily influenced by peat smoke (left), used to dry the malted barley, or by the ex-sherry barrels (right), used to age some whiskies. Additional dimensions, such as lightness or full-bodied richness, are represented on the vertical axis of Table 1. There are some whiskies that use neither peat nor ex-sherry barrels, while some use both. The malt may be dried by means other than peat smoke, such as dry air, and the whisky may be aged in lightly toasted virgin oak, resurfaced ex-bourbon, or heavily charred ex-bourbon barrels with all the residual bourbon-barrel flavors. In general, whiskey can absorb charred smokiness. Although, it's not a scotch whisky, an example of non-peated, charred smokiness can be experienced clearly in the Jack Daniels Old #7 Tennessee Straight Whiskey. With regard to the fruitiness or sherry dimension, whiskey can also be aged in wine or cognac casks which can contribute a range of fruit notes, and rum barrels will add still another dimension entirely, related to sugar, molasses and caramel. The textural aspects of lightness versus fuller body may be most directly related to the types of stills used by the distillery, the variety of oak barrels or wood casks used, and the number of years spent aging or finishing.

We can represent North American whiskeys also along a continuum, as in *Table 2*.

Whiskeys called bourbon contain corn at a minimum of 51%, in the USA, but are likely to contain significantly more. The remaining 49% may be high in, or contain some relative proportions of, corn or wheat or rye or barley. A rye whiskey in the USA has to be at least 51% rye, but, of course, it can be a much higher percent than that, and usually is. Whiskeys can be solely corn or wheat or rye,

TABLE 2
NORTH AMERICAN WHISKEYS

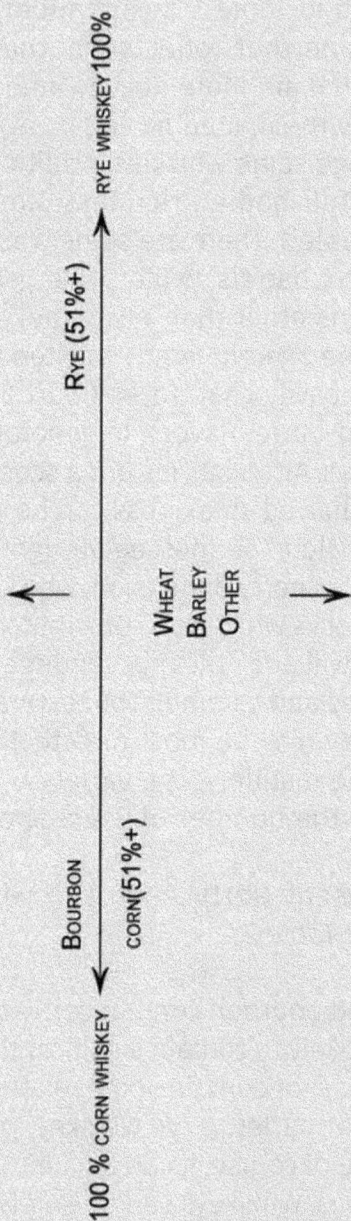

BOURBON   RYE (51%+)
CORN(51%+)

WHEAT
BARLEY
OTHER

100 % CORN WHISKEY   RYE WHISKEY 100%

but those are less common.

Canada doesn't quite fit on our *Table 2* continuum. In Canada, known for its blended, rye whiskies, the base liquor may be corn, or wheat (less common these days), with rye added as a flavoring liquor. It's a bit confusing, but north of the border, that is still considered rye. Also not represented on *Table 2* are exciting, but rare, new, peated American craft whiskeys which we will touch upon later. Peated American whiskeys are of two types, one resembling the Scottish single malt style with a degree of American terroir, the other basically a specialized bourbon .

Regardless, our most immediate goal, for those of you who have never really explored various types of whiskey, is to determine whether you prefer peaty- smoky or fruity-sherried types of scotch whisky. Perhaps, you may be one of the lucky people who already know that you like all kinds of scotch. If you don't already know, here's your chance to find out. With respect to American whiskey and Canadian whisky, you're going to find out if you prefer bourbon that is high corn, high wheat or high rye, or if you prefer rye whiskey more than bourbon. Then you'll be able to dig deeper into a wide variety of whiskeys and chocolates from the sample pairings beginning in Chapter 10 of this book.

When do we get to go shopping? As soon as we make out our shopping lists!

SHOPPING FOR CHOCOLATES

Check out your local gourmet and health food stores for the chocolate bars. These should be plain, dark bars. Please read the labels carefully. No milk chocolate, no milk fat, no special

TABLE 3
CHOCOLATES TO BUY FOR PAIRING PRACTICE

BRAND	TYPE	PROFILE
Valrhona Guanaja 70%	Blend	Fruit & Floral
Madécasse Madagascar 70%	Single Origin	Citrusy Twang
Hoja Verde 70%	Single Origin	Fruit & Spice
The Grenada Company, 71%	Single Origin	Twang & Earth
Lindt, Excellence, 70%	Blend	Fruit & Earth
Green & Blacks, Pure Dark 70%	Blend	Earthy, Fruit & Spice
Theo, Pure Dark 70%	Blend	Naked, Earthy & Spicy
Villakukaya, Esmeraldas, 80%	Single Origin	Naked & Earthy

(NAKED MEANS IT TASTES "CHOCOLATEY" WITHOUT MUCH IN THE WAY OF OTHER FLAVOR NOTES.)

flavorings or added nuts. If the bars contain vanilla, that's okay for our purpose here. If you can't find any of the bars locally, it's possible to purchase them online, particularly on amazon.com. If it's unclear whether these chocolates will be coming directly from the manufacturer, be aware that when buying from a third party, temperature-related damage can occur during shipping. That damage can occur either at the shipping departure point, in transit, or at the reception point. Check weather conditions at both ends and ask whether they provide special weather packing.

Chocolate is best kept between 58 and 68 degrees Fahrenheit (14.44-20 Celsius). Remember that chocolate melts in warm weather, and a white-grayish film or spots, called bloom, can form over the bar's surface. It's safe to eat, but it does affect the flavor and texture. Some bloom is due to cocoa butter fat melting, other (sugar) bloom can occur from condensation and moisture. So, if the temperature is over 70 F (21 C) take a cool bag– an insulated, lunch-type bag– with a plastic- wrapped ice pack inside. Make sure no moisture can escape. The chocolate bar should not be right on top of the ice pack, so add another layer between the two. You don't want it too cold. I like to wind a short sheet of bubble-wrap around the bars, but a small plastic bag should do just fine. When the temperatures plunge below 48 F (8.88 C), I carry the bars in an inside, jacket pocket, with a couple layers of fabric between my body and the bars. Inside a heated environment, I advise removing the bars from the jacket so they don't overheat against the body.

As you can see, some of the chocolate bars listed in the text box entitled "Chocolates to Buy for Pairing Practice," are blends, and the others are single origins. But what is more important is their actual flavor profile. Profiles can vary over time due to changes in cacao bean sourcing, climate conditions, variations in harvests, changes in the fermentation procedures, and production, such as roasting and extended refining. Profiles published here reflect bars made with expiration dates at least through late 2018. After that date, please check my website ctm-chocolate-tasting-meditation.com for any notes on significant changes in profiles. As a minimum, try to buy at least 1 bar that is predominantly Earthy and 1 bar that is Twangy. Others are up to you, but consult the shopping list of whiskeys to make sure you are able to pair.

SHOPPING FOR WHISKEYS

For your trip to the liquor store, try to find one that sells a variety of airplane- size (50ml) sample bottles. If you can't find them, buy yourself stainless steel flasks or small, airtight glass bottles, and head for any good bar. Order a drink, take a sip, and pour the rest in your flask or bottle for take-home. Depending on the laws in your state, you may want to –ahem!– be discreet. Purchase a few of the recommended whiskeys. The ones with an asterisk (*) in front of the name are required to complete the whiskey preference exercise. Whiskeys with (s) in front of their names are substitutes, if you cannot find the recommended ones listed immediately above them. There is no substitute for Maker's Mark that I have seen in the 50 ml size, but it is one of the most widely available bourbons in the world.

Whiskey keeps well as long as it's out of direct sunlight. Avoid freezing temperatures and prolonged exposure in excess of 85 F (29.5 C). It's not nearly as sensitive as chocolate, or wine, so room temperature is usually fine. However, sometimes whiskey will become cloudy if exposed to cold, unless it has gone through a process called cold-filtering. It is said that this filtering reduces flavor notes, so many distillers advertise that their spirits are not cold-filtered

We're going to use the whiskeys with the asterisks(*), or their

Table 4
Whiskeys for Pairing Practice

WHISKEY	PROFILE
*Johnny Walker Black or Red Blended Scotch	Light peat, smoke sherry, malt
*Macallan 12 Year, Sherry Oak (if available)	Full, Sweet, Sherry, Spice
s Chivas Regal Blended Scotch 12 Year	Fruity & Spicy
s Jameson Blended Irish Whiskey	Fruity & Spicy
*Glenlivit 12 Year, single malt (if available)	Light, Sweet, Floral, Spice
s Dewer's White Label Blended Scotch	Light & Fragrant
*Maker's Mark Straight Kentucky Bourbon	High wheat, candied fruit, nut
*Jim Beam, White Label or Devil's Cut, Straight Kentucky Bourbon	High corn, caramel, lemon, wood
s Knob Creek aged 9 Year, Straight Kentucky Bourbon	Spicy, rich & oaky
*Crown Royal, Northern Harvest, Blended Rye	High rye, sweet, mild spice
s Bulleit Frontier Kentucky Straight Bourbon	High rye bourbon
Jack Daniels Old #7 Tennessee Straight Whiskey	High corn, char smoke, sweet,& spice

substitutes (s) listed immediately underneath them, to find your preferred whiskey style. These substitutes by no means replicate the flavors of the ones with the asterisks, but they should be adequate for our purpose. We will then use the easy-to-find chocolates you've just purchased to pair with the best corresponding whiskey. This way, you can get a sense of the process conveniently and affordably, risking little before investing time and cash to hunt down more adventurous chocolate and whiskey pairings that you'll find later in the book.

Johnny Walker Black and Macallan 12 Year, Sherry Oak, represent two ends of the continuum represented in *Table 1* with Chivas Regal, Jameson, Dewars, and Glenlivit, somewhere in between, with little to no smoke, but various notes of fruit, honey, and vanilla. Truth be told, the Johnny Walker is a mildly peated whisky blend, not quite at the far end of the horizontal line in Table 1. If you find that you like the light peat smoke, you can go on later to explore more heavily peated whiskies, such as Connemara or Lagavulin or even some of the new American peated whiskeys. Whereas, if you prefer the Macallan 12 Year, you can go on to explore whiskies that have been aged or finished in sherry or port casks. Highland Park of Orkney Island, northern Scotland, uses both peat and sherry casks. HP cannot be found in small bottles—to my knowledge—and tends to run a bit pricey.

Okay, once you have purchased your chocolate and whiskey, let's learn how to taste them separately, then together.

6

HOW TO TASTE

It is the simplest ritual of my noondays: A square of dark chocolate, little larger than a postage stamp. For its minuteness, I savor it all the more, closing my eyes as it melts gently, generously, in my mouth, as softly exquisite as a kiss.
–Laura Hillenbrand

The proper drinking of Scotch whisky is more than indulgence: it is a toast to civilization, a tribute to the continuity of culture, a manifesto of man's determination to use the resources of nature to refresh mind and body and enjoy to the full the senses with which he has been endowed.
– David Daiches

HERE'S WHAT WE WILL BE LEARNING IN THIS CHAPTER:
1. How to taste chocolate.
2. How to taste whiskey.
3. Identify the whiskey style(s) you prefer.
4. Identify the dark chocolate profile(s) you prefer.

MOST PEOPLE CONSUME CHOCOLATE, rather than taste it. Beyond the first or second bites, the experience may become a blur. We may be highly aware of the tasting experience until our sensory neurons fatigue. Or we may be distracted even for those initial bites. We may simply be consuming automatically and with little consciousness about it. I would suggest that most of us consume rather than taste. Eating is such a primitive process. We can imagine that our prehistoric predecessors evolved watching for danger as they ate. Beyond the first bite, early humans had their eyes fixed on sights and sounds around them, scanning for predators. We learned to approach food by smell, by first impressions. Bitter foods were spit out as suspected toxins. Sweetness we learned to accept from our mother's breast. We learned that some sour flavors were desirable in fermented milk curds or in some tart fruits, others we rejected as spoiled. We began to seek out flavors that were salty, meaty or umami. The ability to slow down, to taste intentionally, to enjoy food, came with the security of created extended families and communities. But the tendency to consume automatically, without paying full attention is the default setting in our brain stems. The ability to savor, to analyze, to store in memory, and to associate and describe flavors are luxuries afforded by the higher-functioning neo-cortex.

Today, we've come to expect enjoyment from our food. When we don't pay much attention to aromas and flavors and textures, we know, on some level, we are cheating ourselves, but we mistakenly think we can compensate by shoveling in more and more. The default setting. Primitive backsliding. What is really needed is to pause, slow down and be in the present moment with the chocolate. We need to tune out distractions so we can attend to the aromas, flavors, and textures of one single piece of chocolate at a time.

.

How to Taste

The best way to learn to taste chocolate is to read the first book in the Deep Tasting Guide ™ series (*Deep Tasting: A Chocolate Lover's Guide To Meditation* ™) and to visit my Chocolate Tasting Meditation website (www.ctm-chocolate-tasting- meditation.com) to listen to audios of the guided tastings.

But sufficient to our purposes here, let me lead you through a brief, generic tasting. You can try this with a bar on the shopping list in Chapter 5, or any of the fine chocolates listed in this book. If you're not an experienced buyer of artisan chocolate, begin with those on the shopping list. It is best to taste chocolate before eating any other foods, or at least a half hour after. Keep in mind that spicy foods and those with strong flavors can influence your taste perceptions even longer. This is why I often say that chocolate is better as an appetizer than a dessert. Also, be careful not to use any scented soap or lotion on your hands. Any fragrance or odors in the environment can throw off your nose.

Before you open a bar of chocolate, take a moment to appreciate the packaging. A lot of thought and money went into creating the presentation. What is the chocolate maker trying to communicate to you? Is the wrapper simple or ornate? Is there a statement about the company's mission or policies? What does the packaging lead you to expect? What emotions surface? Our visual impressions, emotions and expectations impact our smell and taste perceptions. Try to suspend those programmed expectations and taste what's really there in the bar.

See if the bar inside is stylistically consistent with its packaging. There are industrial chocolate companies that spend huge amounts of money on packaging and advertising but deliver impoverished flavor through the use of cheap, commodity cacao and additives. The packaging is designed to elicit emotions and to get you to select that product above any other competing offerings. You know the companies I mean, because you see their products advertised everywhere; they hog all the shelf-space at supermarkets and airports and other places where great chocolate is almost impossible to find, at least in America.

VISUAL

Peel back the foil or open the inner wrapper. Look at the mold design on the bar. Some are very simple and match a minimalist outer packaging. Some bars, with only two ingredients that allow the flavor of the beans to speak for themselves, may be minimalist upon tasting too. But some will surprise you with astonishing complexity. So are there clear, up-front flavors, consistent with the packaging, or something unexpected? Perhaps, a chocolate maker may be going for a rustic style. Is simple packaging with retro or unrefined paper on the outside reflected in less refined textures, perhaps grainy, and undifferentiated flavors in the chocolate itself. Once you taste the chocolate, the flavors may be simple or complex, obvious or subtle. The textures may be smooth, creamy, luxurious, or waxy, or slightly and deliberately grainy. The question is whether the chocolate maker is conveying stylistic consistency that correctly targets the consumers they want. And does the entire product fulfill the expectations of the consumer? That total packaging and product consistency can take years for chocolate makers to achieve.

Some wrappers are elaborate and delicate, works of beauty. I'm a big fan of Soma Chocolate of Toronto, Canada. Fortunately, so are many other people, because, until recently, Soma's outer packaging had been understating their superb chocolate. Despite the simple wrapping, their exquisite mold designs have been pushing their overall quality forward. Truly, Soma has been raising the bar on many fronts for artisan chocolate. The artistry of the mold design on the bar matches their sublime chocolate making. If you are fortunate enough to try one of their bars, you will see that Soma is one of the world's great bar-makers. I just saw a preview of their new packaging, and I'm delighted that the beauty of the mold design is being carried over to the outer wrapping. Now, even someone who doesn't know Soma by reputation will be tempted to buy one of their bars. Whenever tasting new chocolate, be sure to feast your eyes, as well as your nose and taste buds.

What I've said about chocolate packaging goes for whiskey too. I enjoy looking at boxes and bottles of whiskey. Some companies really go all out. Three examples come to mind: Blanton's Single Barrel Bourbon whose iconic, horse-and-jockey bottle stoppers celebrate the Kentucky horse-racing tradition that parallels the rise of bourbon. Distributed by the same company, Caribou Crossing Canadian Whisky sports a metallic caribou on the stopper. And from William Grant & Sons, Monkey Shoulder Blended Single Malt Scotch—love those monkeys! But for now, back to chocolate.

nosing (smelling) chocolate

Preparation.
Keep a pen and paper, or a silenced electronic device, nearby to jot down your impressions of each bar you try. Remember, I suggested you purchase at least 1 bar that had a predominantly earthy profile and 1 with a twang profile. But you can add any others with different profiles.

On a scale of 1(least liked) to 5 (most liked) you will be rating each bar tried. First jot down the flavor profile of the bar, then describe the aromas and flavors you actually discover. Second, you will rate both the aroma and the flavor after the tasting on a scale from 1 to 5, then you will discover the bar's overall score. Later, you will compare the scores you've given each bar and note which one you gave the highest score to determine your flavor profile preference.

Once you open the chocolate, let it breathe 10 minutes or longer. It is highly recommended that you silence any electronic devices, do the tasting in a quiet place, free of distractions, and close your eyes to focus on the inner experience. Be careful to rest your nose and palate between whiffs and tastes. If you have some coffee beans handy, sniffing them for a few seconds between whiffs can help restore your sensory acuity for the nosing exercise.

Before breaking a piece of chocolate, raise the opened bar to your nose. The foil or covering can create an aroma corridor surrounding the chocolate. If you've already broken a piece, raise it to your nose.

What does it smell like? First impressions. Jot them down.
Rest your nose for a few moments, then try again.
Sniff deeper and longer this time.
Any new aromas?
What aroma seems to dominate?
Is it floral?
Or fruity,?
Or nutty?
Or cocoa smelling?

Clear your nose for a half-minute. Jot down your impressions.
Raise the chocolate back up and take another whiff.
Do any other notes appear? Anything you didn't notice before?
Jot down your impressions and rate the aroma from 1 to 5.

After you've completed the Nosing Chocolate exercise, if you're not quite sure what you're smelling, that's okay for now. Some chocolate doesn't have pronounced aromas. Maybe you think it just smells "chocolatey." Or, maybe you think it's more complex than that but you may not be sure what it is you're perceiving. The ability to identify aromas and flavors has to do with experience, memory, and descriptive vocabulary, as well as the sensory input. If you spent your life in Panama and perhaps never tasted a raspberry or blackberry, you won't be able to match a memory to a descriptor. In the chapter on flavor, you will be presented with descriptors to jog your sense memories. You will find new ways to identify aromas and flavors of both chocolate and whiskey. For now, just do the best you can. Note the name of the bar and jot down what you smell and taste. When you get to Chapter 8, The Amazing World of Aroma and Flavor, you can try this exercise again with the same bar and with the Chocolopolis Chocolate Aroma & Flavor Wheel and my Chocolate Aroma/Flavor Profile Inventory in front of you. You may be surprised at the difference in your two experiences.

tasting

When you've finished smelling the chocolate, place a piece of it–about a half inch square– in your mouth. Don't bite the chocolate, just let it slowly melt on your tongue. Keep your mouth slightly open and occasionally draw air in through your teeth during the tasting. Give the piece of chocolate about 10 seconds to begin melting, then...

What is the first thing you taste? Is it a big hit of sweetness? Is it sugary, syrupy or like caramel or molasses? Or is it simply like fruit? If so, what kind of fruit? What flavor emerges next?

Or is it nutty? Roasted or raw nut? What kind of nut?

Or are there spicy or herbal flavors?

Or does it taste like cocoa powder?
What flavors emerge next?
Do the flavors emerge one by one, sequentially, or as if stacked on upon the other?
Feel the texture as it spreads out and coats your tongue.
Is the melting creamy or buttery? Clumpy or thin?
Move your tongue around.
Gently push the chocolate up and stroke it against your hard palate.
Then let the chocolate sit and melt again on your tongue.
Let each flavor emerge in turn.
Note again if the flavors appear sequentially, one after another or stacked one upon the other.
Do you experience different flavors in different parts of your mouth?
Follow the unfolding flavors until the chocolate entirely melts.
Now you may be into the aftertaste.
How is this chocolate finishing? Sweet, sour, bitter? Acidic?
What does it taste like?
Stay with it, allowing the residual flavors to unfold.
The entire tasting process– from start until no discernible after-taste can be detected– can take at least 5 minutes. You may want to jot down the flavor notes you were able to discern.

Remember to rate the flavor using a scale of 1(least liked) to 5 (most liked

When you finish the piece of chocolate for each bar, jot down your impressions. Add the scores for the aroma and flavor for each bar. Divide by 2 to get the overall rating for that bar. Then after tasting other bars, compare. Which bar did you give the highest score? Check the shopping list in Chapter 5, if it was one of those bars, or wherever it was first listed in this book. What flavor profile was it supposed to have? Given the dominant flavors and any subdominant note you were able to detect, does the flavor profile make sense? If not, perhaps it will after you've had a chance to work with Chapter 8. When you finish each bar, note the score you gave it and any impressions you jotted down. Which of the bars did you score the highest? Check the bar's flavor profile. For now, that is your flavor profile preference.

You can repeat the Nosing and Tasting exercises after waiting about 10 minutes. If switching to another bar, make sure you permit your taste buds time to refresh. You can sip some plain warm water, or chew a plain, unsalted cracker to clean your palate. An unsalted, unflavored rice cake can also be used. The International Chocolate Awards uses a bland polenta. At ICA, the judges are tasting large numbers of chocolates within a short time period during these competitions, and they have found it works for them over the years. When tasting at home, I prefer an unsalted blue-corn chip. Whatever you use, take care not to allow particles to become lodged in your teeth so as not to influence taste. Bite the cracker or chip into coarse bits and move them about your tongue, spit them out, then swish more water around in your mouth. And you're ready to go.

Experiment! As long as the restorative is unflavored, find one that is most effective for you. What if you don't favor one flavor profile over another? What if you have no preference? Well, lucky you! I like them all, too. I find that my preferences change from time to time, but they are all dear to my heart. My main concern is how well the particular flavor profile is interpreted through the chocolate maker's amazing, alchemical skills.

A shot of whiskey is approximately 1.5 oz or 44.3 ml. That's too much to pour for our purposes. A small shot is about 1 oz (30 ml). A dram is technically 1/8 oz (3.697 ml) but "dram" is not usually used literally. When someone asks for a dram of whiskey, they expect a fair serving that is a shot or more. For our purposes, anywhere between .5 oz (14.7868 ml) to 1 oz (29.57 ml) is fine. You should get approximately 3 small servings from those 50 ml bottles for the tastings in this chapter. At least, I do.

After selecting a whiskey, pour about .5-1 oz (14.8-30 ml) into a small fluted wine glass or a Glencairn-type glass (pictured on the book cover). I advise against the use of a whiskey tumbler for our purposes here since we want the aromas to rise up to our nose rather than disperse. We will be tasting our whiskeys "straight up" or "neat," that is, without the addition of water, club soda or anything else. The whiskey tumbler served in bars is meant to accommodate ice and other liquids, such as club soda, ginger ale, tonic water, and so on. In general, there's nothing wrong with drinking your whiskey that way or anyway you like it. Just for the purpose of this book, we are simply sampling, tasting without dilution or alteration rather than "drinking."

We need to let whiskey breathe. As you hopefully experienced in Chapter 4, whiskey changes as it breathes. Environmental factors in the room, the strength, and the age of the whiskey may affect optimal time for allowing the alcohol to evaporate while the aromas and flavors release. I usually let my whiskey sit anywhere from 15 to 20 minutes. Experts say to let whisky breathe 1 minute for every year in the barrel or cask. For the whiskeys on our shopping list, 15 minutes should be more than sufficient. While we will be exploring aroma and flavor in greater depth later in this chapter, I will briefly guide you by asking questions to orient you to the whiskey tasting experience. You may find it helpful to jot down notes about each of these tastings. Note which whiskeys you like or don't to help you recall which styles you prefer. Also, identify as many aromas and flavors as you discover, even in these preliminary explorations. Perhaps, you will not be able to describe what you smell and taste at this point. By keeping notes on your tastings, you may be able to look back later and appreciate how you've progressed.

how to taste whiskey

You may wish to consult one of the flavor wheels and use the appropriate whiskey inventory form from Chapter 8.

1.   Visual. Hold the glass up to the light and examine the color. Is it a light golden wheat color or a deeper gold? Or is it closer to amber? The deeper the color, the longer it's been aged, unless caramel coloring has been added (legal in Scotland, other places not). Can you detect any hints of pink? Aging or finishing in a sherry cask may contribute a pinkish cast. There are camps that say not to swirl the glass or warm it with your hand and those who believe otherwise. As I become more experienced in these matters, I may change my mind, but I keep my bottles at room tempera- ture and just let the whiskey sit in the glass to breathe. I usually give the liquid a gentle, half swirl, then look to see whether the whiskey has "legs." Does the liquid seem thin or create heavier, slow-moving fingers as it runs back down to join the rest pooled in the bottom of the glass? Supposedly, thicker, slower legs indicate increased body and texture from aging and wood tannins. But Karen Best, citing the ongoing controversy, put legs to an informal test and challenged their significance in a recent article for whiskeywash.com. She stated that, perhaps, legs only tell us about higher alcohol content, information readily available in the modern era right on the bottle's label.

2.   Nosing. Slowly lower your nose to just above the rim of the glass for a brief sniff. Be careful not to burn your nose. Keep your mouth slightly opened. (I always have trouble remembering this.) You may note the alcohol still dominates as it rises up and evaporates, but perhaps you can catch hints of other aromas, such as florals or delicate fruits. Set the glass down and let it sit a few minutes. While trying to determine the optimal time to let your whiskey breathe, take a whiff every five minutes or so and note when the whiskey aromas seem to stabilize and the alcohol has moved out of the way.

Once the whiskey has breathed, raise the glass and tilt it almost horizton- ally to your nose. Nose more centrally between the upper and lower rims this time, smell the liquid as it pools on the side of the glass. Whiff it again and see if you can describe the aromas. You may wish to jot down notes or wait until a later nosing and tasting.

While the whiskey is still lying on the side of the glass, move your nose down toward the bottom rim. You may detect heavier compounds, such as the earthy, smoky, woody and spicy notes. Pull your nose back and jot down any notes, if you wish.

how to taste whiskey

Slowly raise your nose just about level to the top of the glass rim. Does it smell like malt or grain? Jot down any notes .

As you bring your nose up, over the glass, are you passing through winey, fruity or floral notes? Make any notes, if you wish.

Rest your nose a few minutes. Try again.

Nose over the lower rim, do you pick up smoky, nutty or honey or caramel notes? Do you detect vanilla or any other spices, like ginger or pepper? On top of the rim again. Any fruit notes? If so, are they citrusy, or orchard fruits like apple or pear, or any other kind of fruits? Are they fresh or dry fruits?
After you nose the whiskey, remember to make notes on the perceived aromas. And, most importantly at this point, did you like the aroma of the whisky?
Write down the name of the whiskey, rate your liking of the aroma, 1 (least liked) to 5 (most liked). You will do that for each whiskey you try to determine your whiskey style.

3.   Tasting. As you take your first sip, you can ask these questions about flavor again. See if you find any of them on the palate this time. You can also use the checklists in the Chapter 8.

Sip with a slight suck to aerate or aerate it on a chew. First impression. Is the whiskey sweet or "dry?" Allow the whiskey to coat your tongue, chew the whiskey a little to explore the texture. Gently suck air in to aerate and see what flavors show up. Keep in mind that you have the option of spitting when doing a tasting. But if you swallow, open your mouth slightly and breathe outward over the whiskey. Is it smooth or harsh or creamy whiskey? What flavors do you detect?

If swallowing, what flavors emerge on the finish? Was the flavor substantial and evenly distributed, gradually thin, or just suddenly drop off? In other words, was the finish short, medium or long? After you taste the whiskey, remember to make notes on perceived flavors. And, most importantly at this point, did you like the whiskey? Rate your liking for the flavor, 1 (least liked) to 5 (most liked). Then add your aroma score to your flavor score, and divide by 2 to determine your overall rating of the tasting sample from 1-5. You will compare this score to others you rated to discover the highest rated score—your preferred whiskey style.

Now that you know a little about nosing and tasting whiskey, let's take these new skills out for a run to get a rough idea of your preferred whiskey style. Try the whiskey Trials 1-5 in the textboxes with a time interval of at least 10 minutes or more between each one to give your nose and palate time to refresh. It is advisable to drink water after each tasting. There's no reason to try more than one trial on the same day. Take your time, make your observations, jot down your notes, assign them scores, and above all else... enjoy!

whiskey trials

TRIAL 1: SCOTCH–FRUITY OR SHERRIED

Following the directions for nosing and sipping, begin at the sherried (Macallan12) or fruity (Chivas Regal 12) end of the continuum. If neither of these are available, try Jameson Blended Irish Whiskey. Did you like any of these? Jot down a few notes about what you smelled or tasted and what you liked about it. Rate it on a scale of 1 to 5 for your liking of aroma, then flavor, then add them and divide by 2 to get an average for overall preference of the sample on a scale of 1 to 5.

TRIAL 2: SCOTCH–SMOKY OR PEATY

Now to the other end of the spectrum, the smoky type. Following the procedure for nosing and sipping, try the Johnny Walker Black or Red label. Did you like either of these? Jot down a few notes about what you smelled or tasted and what you liked about it. Rate it for your liking for aroma, then flavor, then overall preference of the sample on a scale of 1 to 5.

SUMMARY:

Which scotch style did you prefer? The fruity/sherried type or the smoky/peaty type? Referring to your rating scale should help you answer this question. Make a note of your preference. As we present various categories of whiskeys, you may choose to explore some of those brands and try suggested pairings with the chocolate.

Now let's see which category of mainstream North American whiskeys you might prefer. Follow the same procedures for nosing and sipping. Remember to jot down impressions as you go along.

whiskey trials

TRIAL 3: CLASSIC HIGH CORN CONTENT BOURBON–JIM BEAM WHITE LABEL

Jot down a few notes about what you smelled or tasted. What did you like or not like about it? Rate it for aroma and flavor on a scale of 1 to 5. Rate your averaged impression on a scale of 1 to 5.

TRIAL 4: HIGH WHEAT CONTENT BOURBON—MAKER'S MARK S IV, STRAIGHT KENTUCKY BOURBON

Jot down a few notes about what you smelled or tasted and what you liked about it. Rate it for aroma and flavor on a scale of 1 to 5. Rate your averaged, overall impression on a scale of 1 to 5.

TRIAL 5: RYE OR HIGH RYE CONTENT BOURBON—CROWN ROYAL NORTHERN HARVEST RYE WHISKEY OR
BULLEIT FRONTIER KENTUCKY STRAIGHT BOURBON.

Canadian rye tends to be smoother than US rye. The Bulleit is a high rye bourbon. Jot down a few notes about what you smelled or tasted and what you liked about it. Rate it for aroma and flavor on a scale of 1 to 5. Rate your averaged, overall impression from 1 to 5.

SUMMARY:

Which one, or ones, did you prefer? Refer to your rating scales to help you answer this question. Make a note of your preference among the mainstream North American whiskey categories. As we present various categories of whiskeys, you may choose to explore some of those brands and suggested pairings with the chocolates.

Tasting Whiskey and Chocolate Together

Now that you've discovered your whiskey style(s) and chocolate preference(s), set that information aside for now. We are going to try the suggested pairs for tasting chocolate and whiskey together. Your preferences at this stage may not correspond to those pairings. But that's okay. These are just training exercises. Just try whichever pairings you can that are listed in this chapter. If you're one of those lucky people who like all kinds of whiskeys and all kinds of chocolates, you can try as many of these chocolate and whiskey pairings as you like, later on.

Pre-Tasting Guidelines

Refer to the textbox labeled *Chocolate Paired with Whiskey*. Note the key at the bottom. Familiarize yourself with both the chocolate and the whiskey of each pairing independently by screening them with the nosing and sipping procedures. Clear your palate with a few sips of water, then wait a few minutes before trying the tasting together. When doing a pairing, taste the chocolate first, then move to the whiskey. Chocolate flavors can be subtle and delicate, so experience the flavors and textures of the chocolate first. Let the rich cocoa butter coat your tongue. Whiskey is stronger, more robust. See how they interact and how they finish

There are two ways to do these tasting pairs.

1.   Sequentially. Taste a piece of chocolate, let it melt completely, then sip the whiskey after.

2.   Simultaneously. While the chocolate is still melting in your mouth, take a sip of the whiskey, thereby, mixing the two in your mouth, allowing them to interact and influence one another to a greater degree than the sequential method.

For the data collection informing this book, both the sequential and simultaneous methods were used. The simultaneous method was heavily relied upon as that was judged to be the more rigorous test of compatibility. Using this method, unique, additional flavors, as well as off notes, jumped to the foreground.

Jot down a description and reaction after trying the chocolate, the whiskey, then after trying them as a pairing. Note the flavor profiles of both the chocolate and the whiskey. Jot down your impressions. Did you like the combination? Rate each pair you try on a scale of 1 to 5. Knowing your reaction to each pair will help you choose others of their flavor profile categories that are similar, if you liked the pair, or dissimilar, if you didn't

Chocolate Paired with Whiskey

Chocolate	Flavor Profile	Whiskey	Flavor Profile
Pairing 1 - CHOCOLATE WITH SHERRIED OR FRUITY WHISKY			
Valrhona, Guanaja 70%	FF	Macallan 12 Year, Sherry Oak	A (W/S)
or Madecasse, Madagascar 70%	T		
OR			
Madecasse, Madagascar 70%	T	Chivas Regal Blended Scotch 12 Year	B1 (B)
Pairing2 Chocolate with **Peated whisky**			
Hoja Verde, dark 72%	Fr&S	Johnny Walker Black Label	B4 (B)
Madecasse, Madagascar 70%	T		
Pairing 3-CHOCOLATE WITH CLASSIC, HIGH CORN BOURBON			
Madecasse, Madagascar 70%	Fr&S	Jim Beam, Kentucky Straight Bourbon	NAM1
Theo Dark 70%	T	or Jim Beam Devil's Cut	
or			
Green & Blacks, Pure Dark 70%	E&Fr&S		
Pairing 4-CHOCOLATE WITH HIGH WHEATED BOURBON			
Madecasse Madagascar 70%	T	Maker's Mark	NAM2 (B) N2 (P)
or Green & Blacks 70%	N&E&S		
Pairing 5 –CHOCOLATE WITH RYE OR HIGH RYE BOURBON			
Green & Blacks 70%	E&Fr&S	Crown Royal, Northern Harvest Rye	N3 (P)
or Villakukaya, Esmeraldas 80%	T	Bulleit Frontier Kentucky Straight Bourbon	
OR			
Theo Dark 70%	E&Fr&S		

Key
Chocolate:
E=Earthy; Fr=Fruit; Fl=Floral; FF=Fruit & Floral; T=Citrusy Twang; S=Spices & H=Herbs N=Naked ("chocolatey" un-nuanced)
Profiles from the C-spot®; updated, Peluso, R. M.
Whisky: from (W/S) Wishart/Selfbuilt's WhiskyAnalysis.com; (B) Broom, D; modifications, Peluso, R. M. (P)

7

WHERE CHOCOLATE AND
WHISKEY GET THEIR FLAVORS

"A good malt bears the imprint of its origins. The source of the water, the quality of the air, and the character of the peat used to dry the malted barley, all combine to make something unique–the very essence of its environment. Malt whisky is like the Scots' tongue – broadly one language yet, within that, so many different dialects, each one unique to its own distillery. It is this subtle distinction which gives every malt its unmistakable identity."
– Highland Park Distillery brochure

"Flavor beans dazzle with their complexity. The very best among them, the ones that have been treated wisely, offer an exhilarating ride for the taste buds…"
–Maricel E. Presilla

TERROIR

THIS TERM IS BANDIED ABOUT in both the chocolate and whiskey worlds. It's been borrowed from the wine industry, where the concept is, perhaps, just a little less complicated. A simple explanation of terroir is the unique environment (soil, wind, rainfall, temperature, sunlight, ecosystem, traditional handling) that contributes to the flavor of the final product. In actuality, this is rather complex for chocolate, and even more so for whiskey. Chocolate and whiskey share more than you might think, for example, both depend upon fermentation and yeast to develop their aromatics and flavors. Let's take a look at how those elements among others shape the sensory aspects of chocolate and whiskey.

FLAVOR PRE-CURSORS IN CACAO AND CHOCOLATE

What contributes to the flavor of chocolate? The genetics and growing conditions of the cacao trees and their fruit—the pods—which contain pulp and seeds (cacao beans). Then post-harvesting treatment: the fermentation and drying procedures. These steps thus far contribute to the notion of terroir in chocolate. Before shipping, distribution, and chocolate production can begin, you either have adequate to good or inadequate beans. To sum up the potential confronting the chocolate maker: You cannot make good chocolate from bad beans, but you can sure mess up good beans with bad chocolate-making. So much for terroir, but flavor development doesn't stop there.

Assuming the cacao pods and beans (seeds) are extracted at the proper maturity, fermentation needs to be of adequate duration for each variety of bean and the optimal duration and methods need to be known by the farmers or the cacao cooperatives in charge of fermentation. This knowledge was usually passed down, but increasingly cacao technologists are bringing more information, method and consistency into the process. Traditionally, the beans, still dripping with pulp that surrounds them within the pod, are placed in wooden boxes and covered with banana leaves. Temperatures build up as the natural sugars in the pulp begin the fermentation process. During this time a series of chemical processes take place.

Lacking oxygen, the temperature begins to climb to 80º- 90ºF (32º - 38ºC) in 1-2 days. This activates yeasts (single-cell fungi), such as Saccharomyces cerevisiae (brewer's yeast), as well as others found on the cacao pods and environmental surfaces, including human hands. Through enzymatic breakdown, the sugars of the pulp decompose to form simpler fructose and glucose, carbon dioxide, and ethanol (same as occurs in the fermentation stages of wine, beer, and yes, whiskey). The stage is now set for bacteria, such as acetobacter or lactobacter, to launch the next stage of fermentation.

During the second stage, in which temperatures can reach around 120ºF (49º C), the process continues for up to 5 more days, approximately. Oxygen is introduced as the beans are periodically turned. This both decreases the chance for mold formation and evens the fermentation throughout. The alcohol oxidizes; lactic acid and acetic acid (vinegar) are formed. The heat and action of the acids slowly penetrates and breaks down the cell walls of the beans. These processes permit the rise of fruity esters which enter the bean and contribute to precursors of aroma and flavor. Enzymes interact with cacao proteins to produce peptides and amino acids which enable polyphenols, along with the alkaloids theobromine and caffeine, leading to chocolate's bitterness and astringency. The oxidation process also causes a browning of cacao beans that gives chocolate its characteristic color.

Once the fermentation process is complete, the beans must be dried, neither too slowly nor too rapidly. The drying takes place in the tropical sun. Sometimes, artificial drying is employed, and if this process produces fumes or smoke, off notes may be introduced. Drying too rapidly results in the bean husks trapping water inside, and this can result in mold. In addition, care must be taken to avoid exposing the beans to external sources of moisture—not easy in a rainforest. So some form of drying shed or covering is used. On the other hand, if drying is too slow, acetic acid builds up. Like Goldilocks, the beans need conditions that are just right. To achieve consistent results takes expertise, and increasingly, scientific input and training are being brought to cacao farmers and farm cooperatives.

The dry beans must then be properly bagged and shipped, without being subjected to fumes or moisture along the way, and arrive at their destination, whether that be a distributor or the end-user chocolate maker, in good condition. The beans must be properly stored, in a cool, dry area, to prevent moth or other pest infestation. Cacao beans will absorb odors, so storage areas must eliminate exposure.

Odor compounds arising during the fermentation process that contribute to chocolate aroma have been extensively studied. Not being chemistry-oriented myself, I tend to glaze over during these discussions. However, Aprotosoaie, Luca and Miron published an overview of aromatic compounds found by several researchers. Note how specific some of these perceptual effects can be for particular compounds. Also see how often more than one compound gives rise to similar aromas. Aromas, such as, cocoa or chocolate, nutty, fruity, and floral tend to show up frequently. This seeming redundancy suggests to me a robust tendency toward distinctive aromatic/

flavor profiles. It also points to the possibility of manipulating the process to encourage certain compounds over others, and some companies are indeed now attempting to "build a better bean" with such intervention, for better or for worse. We will see.

Aprotosoaie et al. (2016)

COMPOUND   AROMA

ALCOHOLS & PHENOLS

Compound	Aroma
1-Propanol	Light peat, smoke sherry, malt
2-Methyl-1-butanol	Full, Sweet, Sherry, Spice
2,3-Butanediol	Fruity & Spicy
2-Pentanol	Fruity & Spicy
1-Hexanol	Light, Sweet, Floral, Spice
2-Hexanol	Light, Sweet, Floral, Spice
Trans-3-hexen-1-ol	Light & Fragrant
2-Heptanol	High wheat, candied fruit, nut
1-Phenylethanol	High corn, caramel, lemon, wood
2-Phenylethanol	Spicy, rich & oaky
Benzyl alcohol	High rye, sweet, mild spice

ALDEHYDES AND KETONES

Compound	Aroma
2-Phenyl acetaldehyde	Honey, floral
2-Methylpropanal	Chocolate (sweet)
2-Phenylpropanal	Floral
2-Methylbutanal	Chocolate (sweet), dark chocolate, malty
3-Methylbutanal	Chocolate (sweet), dark chocolate, malty
2-Phenyl-2-butenal	Chocolate (sweet)
4-Methyl-2-phenyl-2-pentenal	Cocoa, chocolate (sweet)
n-Hexanal	Green, herbal
5-Methyl-2-phenyl-2-hexenal	Cocoa, chocolate (sweet)
2-Nonenal	Green, herbal
Vanillin	Chocolate, sweet, vanilla
2-Pentanone	Fruity
2-Heptanone	Fruity, floral
Acetophenone	Floral
2-Hydroxy acetophenone	Heavy floral, herbal
4-Methyl acetophenone	Fruity, floral

Aprotosoaie et al. (2016)

Acids

2-Methylpropionic acid	Floral
3-Phenylpropionic acid	Sweet, rose
2,3-Butanediol	Honey, floral
Ethyl acetate	Pineapple, fruity
Isobutyl acetate	Fruity
Isoamyl acetate	Fruity, banana
Benzyl acetate	Floral, jasmine
Methylphenyl acetate	Sweet, honey, jasmine
Ethylphenyl acetate	Fruity, sweet, floral
2-Phenylethyl acetate	Honey, floral
Ethyl butyrate	Pineapple, fruity
Ethyl lactate	Fruity
Diethyl succinate	Pleasant aroma, floral
Ethyl 2-methylbutanoate	Fruity
Ethyl 3-methylbutanoate	Fruity
Ethyl valerate	Fruity, apple
Ethyl hexanoate	Fruity
Ethyl octanoate	Fruity, floral
Ethyl decanoate	Fruity, pear, grape
Ethyl laurate	Fruity, floral
Isoamyl benzoate	Balsamic, sweet, floral
Methyl salicylate	Bitter-almond, nutty
Methyl cinnamate	Balsamic, strawberry
Ethyl cinnamate	Sweet, cinnamon-like, sweet chocolate

Amines, amides, nitriles, purines

Benzonitrile	Almond, nutty
N-(2-phenethyl) formamide	Essences, floral

Lactones

δ-Octenolactone	Coconut, nutty
γ-Decalactone	Peach, fruity

TERPENOIDS

Geraniol	Floral, rose, fruity
Geranyl acetate	Floral, rose, lavender
α-Terpenyl formate	Herbal, citrus, fruity
Linalool (cis-pyranoid)	Floral, green, herbal
Linalool (trans-pyranoid)	Floral
Linalool oxide (cis-furanoid)	Nutty
Linalool oxide (trans-furanoid)	Floral, citrus, fruity

FURANS, FURANONES, PYRANS, PYRONES

2-Furfural	Almond, nutty
5-Methyl-2-furfural	Sweet caramel, sweet chocolate
2-Furfuryl acetate	Fruity, banana
2-Acetylfuran	Sweet chocolate, balsamic, slightly coffee
2-Acetyl-5-methylfuran	Strong nutty
2-Furfuryl propionate	Spicy, floral
5-(1-Hydrohyethyl)-2-furanone	Red fruit, jam, green notes (fruity & herbal)
Dihydro-3-hydroxy-4,4-dimethyl-2-furanon	Coconut,, nutty
4-Hydroxy-2,5-dimethyl-3-furanone (furaneol	Fruity, strawberry, hot sugar, nuts
3-Hydroxy-2-methyl-4-pyrone (maltol	Roasted nuts, nutty
5,6-Dihydro-6-pentyl-2-pyrone	Coconut, nutty

PYRROLES

Pyrrole	Nutty
2-Acetylpyrrole	Chocolate (sweet), hazelnut
Pyrrole-2-carboxaldehyde	Nutty

PYRAZINES

2-Methylpyrazine	Nutty, sweet chocolate, cocoa, roasted nuts
2-Ethylpyrazine	Peanut butter, musty, nutty
2,5-Dimethylpyrazine	Cocoa, nutty, sweet chocolate
2,6-Dimethylpyrazine	Nutty, coffee, green, herbal
2-Ethyl-5-methylpyrazine	Nutty, raw potato
2,3-Diethylpyrazine	Nutty, hazelnut, cereal
2,3-Dimethylpyrazine	Caramel, cocoa, sweet chocolate
2,3,5-Trimethylpyrazine	Earthy, cocoa, sweet choco., roasted nuts, peanut
2,3,5,6-Tetramethylpyrazine	Chocolate, cocoa, coffee, mocha
2,3,5-Trimethyl-6-ethylpyrazine	Candy, sweet chocolate

FLOW CHART: FROM TREE TO POST-HARVEST

GROWING ⟶ HARVESTING ⟶ SEPARATING PULP & BEANS FROM POD ⟶ FERMENTATION ⟶
DRYING ⟶ PACKING ⟶ SHIPPING ⟶ STORAGE/DISTRIBUTION

Now it's the chocolate maker's turn to influence flavor. What happens during chocolate-making? Storage, sorting, roasting, winnowing (shell removal), grinding and refining to reduce the beans to a fluid called "chocolate liquor" (no, not the alcohol kind). Then, sugar or other ingredients may be added, followed by conching (further refining), storing and aging, tempering (or crystallization), molding, wrapping and packaging. What can go wrong? Plenty!

Let's break it down. Have a look at the flow chart.

FLOW CHART: CHOCOLATE-MAKING ACTIVITIES

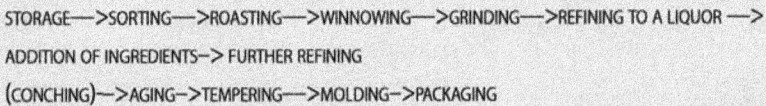

STORAGE—>SORTING—>ROASTING—>WINNOWING—>GRINDING—>REFINING TO A LIQUOR —>
ADDITION OF INGREDIENTS—> FURTHER REFINING
(CONCHING)—>AGING—>TEMPERING—>MOLDING—>PACKAGING

Assuming the beans were properly stored and are in good condition, the chocolate-making process begins with sorting, then roasting the beans. There are many ways to roast, and most chocolate makers have their signature styles. During roasting, amino acids brown and reduce sugars to enhance the chocolate color. This is known as the Maillard Reaction.

This reaction converts tannins and reduces bitterness and astringency in the chocolate. It also produces aromatic chemicals, such as aldehydes, that contribute to flavor formation.

The next steps are shell removal (winnowing) then breaking down and refining the nibs (the nuts remaining after the shell is removed) to form chocolate liquor, then conching to further refine the liquor. During the refining and conching stages, the cocoa nibs will be crushed and broken down in a series of ways, from rollers to stone grinders, and through further churning, called conching, to affect aroma, flavor, and the way the chocolate texture will feel in the mouth (mouthfeel). It is also during refining that sugar and other ingredients may be added and particle size continues to be reduced. Finally, during conching the chocolate reaches a desired particle fineness (measured in microns) to achieve a smooth and melty quality. Conching removes residual moisture, acetic acid and other volatile chemicals. Therefore, it contributes to flavor development by releasing and amplifying favorable aromatics. Here's where the chocolate maker's skill comes into play in order to avoid under-conching, as well as over-conching. Under-conching results in a grainier-feeling chocolate that doesn't melt in an even manner. Over-conching can remove too much of the desirable aromatic and flavor notes, also rendering the chocolate overly smooth to the point of clumpiness. Once the chocolate liquor emerges from conching, it will harden at room temperature. Chocolate makers can store it at that consistency to age it, or temper it and use it right away. In freshly made chocolate, particularly that which is made with only cacao mass, sugar, and additional cocoa butter, flavors will shift over time. That can happen while the chocolate is stored away, or if not aged, it will continue after it is tempered and molded into chocolate bars, even as it's en route to the consumer. The chocolate maker has to anticipate how soon the consumer is likely to pick up a bar and whether that might occur before beneficial changes in flavor have had a chance to manifest.

FLAVOR IN WHISKY AND WHISKEY

What contributes to the flavor of whiskey? The notion of terroir is even more complex in whiskey-making because many ingredients–the grain and malted barley–and the barrels in which the whiskey matures, do not necessarily originate in the regions where the whiskey is made. Only a few Scottish distillers actually use grain grown in their immediate location or create their own malt these days. Yet, there are scotch whiskies that are astonishingly evocative of place. I'm thinking, in particular, of the whiskies from the islands off the coast of western Scotland, such as Islay, and their marine aromas.

There is some effort among craft distillers to reflect their region. Westland Distillery in Seattle is coming closer day by day. There are others. While not all truly reflect terroir, the current trend is in keeping with ideals of sustainability, to buy, eat and drink locally. An increasing number of distilleries produce expressions that are uniquely theirs, that have the stamp of their own personality or style upon their whiskeys. And many of these distilleries tend to use local grain.

One of the most important aspects of distillery location has always been the water source, its purity and mineral composition. Distilleries like to brag about their water sources and protected natural springs. In Kentucky, bourbon producers tout their hard, limestone water. In Scotland, however, soft water is preferred because it keeps the ph down and provides minerals that aid in fermentation. Water may be one of the most salient components of terroir; the others are the air and climate. Temperature influences the rate of maturation. The warmer the weather, the quicker the aging in the barrel. Additionally, what's in the air? Is it clean, dry, mountain air, or humid sea air whose saline aroma will permeate the barrel and flavor of the whiskey?

But the grain, the malted barley, the yeast, are they local? Where do they come from? If not sourced locally, how can they be said to be constituents of terroir? Where do the barrels come from in which the whiskey is aged? With maturation in wood said to contribute between 60-80 % of flavor, how can we talk about terroir if you're using American white oak, ex-bourbon barrels, or Spanish oak and Spanish ex-sherry casks in the Scottish Highlands? As you can probably see right here, the concept of terroir becomes exceedingly complex. Terroir? Whose terroir? How much is terroir? Which components?

There are significant differences in the preparation of whiskeys. The schematics below are simplified overviews of the respective processes to describe how a single malt varies from a bourbon. Without burdening the reader with a lot of technical information, I want to give you a sense of when and where flavors are introduced or modified.

SINGLE MALTS

FLOW CHART FOR MAKING SINGLE MALT WHISKY

BARLEY—>WATER ADDED—> PARTIAL GERMINATION OR "MALTING"—>DRYING OVER DRY AIR OR KILNING OVER PEAT FIRE—>MILLING TO GRIST (FLOUR)—>HOT WATER ADDED—>MASHING TO PRODUCE "WORT"—> FERMENTATION OF WORT WITH YEAST TO PRODUCE "BEER"—>DISTILLATION 1—>DISTILLATION 2 (CONDENSING)—>CUT POINTS—>MATURATION IN OAK BARRELS OR CASKS—>FINISHING IN CASKS—> BOTTLING

There are a few pivotal points, flavor-wise, beyond the selection of the water and the grain, that are critical in creating unique flavor. One is how the malt is dried, whether using a neutral air drying or peat fire. The next critical point is the yeasting and fermenting. Yeast, as we saw in the case of cacao, causes a series of chemical reactions, among them, the sugar conversion that results in a low alcohol content "beer" that then goes on to be distilled. Yeast strains directly influence the flavor, and their identities may be closely held proprietary information. The "beer" produced during fermentation is then distilled, and through evaporation and condensation, the alcohol content is boosted. The number of times the beer is distilled and the type of equipment used is critical. Taller, longer stills and piping tend to produce a lighter whisky. A long, slow distillation in copper stills may result in floral and grassy notes. If you want to know more about stills, that information is readily available online. In many cases, distilleries show off their stills on their websites.

After distillation, the next critical step is the "cut point." This is when the master- distillers decide where, in the stream of whiskey emerging from the still, they will choose the spirit that will go on to aging. There's a quality difference between the beginning, middle and end of the emerging spirit. A perfect illustration of this selection process is the practice of the master distiller at The Macallan to only take 16% of the output to go on to age. So, the master distiller decides what qualities to put up to age and where to locate them in the stream of spirit, then the spirit with those qualities is selected as it emerges from the still, then cut (separated) from the rest.

The alcohol by volume, or ABV, is expressed as a percentage. Laws govern the limits of alcohol strength that can go into the barrel. Unless released as barrel strength, the distillery will dilute the whisky to achieve a target strength. The bottles disclose the final alcohol content. If expressed as alcohol by volume, double it to get the "proof." For example, if the ABV is 45 %, you're buying a whisky that is 90 proof. And that percentage is another factor in flavor. There's a big difference in a whisky that is 80 or 90 proof or higher.

But what do the experts say is the biggest component of flavor? Between 60-80% happens during maturation in the barrel and cask. Think of that! The majority of flavor is said to be created after the "white dog" (fresh, clear whisky right out of the still) is placed in the barrel. Scotch must be aged a minimum of 3 years. It can be aged in ex-bourbon American white oak or virgin, toasted oak. Or it can be aged in ex-sherry casks (the older, traditional method) or ex-port, wine, cognac, or rum casks. All these aging environments will impart different aromatic and flavor notes. This is the art of the master distiller—to decide how long to mature a whisky, in which barrels and casks, and in how many casks. In addition, where the barrels are placed in the warehouse and the climate conditions, contribute to the flavor profiles that develop during maturation.

The flavor finishing in various casks can be quite protracted and complicated. And that's why an old scotch can command such high prices. In the case of scotch, it is more than just paying for taking up warehouse space; it is the meticulous monitoring and creative intervention of the master distillers. And by the way, the age stated on the label reflects the minimum age of all the whisky that goes into the final product. Remember that the term "single malt" simply means that all the whisky in the bottle was made at the same distillery. But the master distiller may be mixing (marrying) the contents of barrels that have been aged 10 years plus 12 years plus, possibly, even older whisky to achieve the flavor results desired. But the label will only state 10 years.

AMERICAN WHISKEY

Below is a basic flow chart of the procedures followed for making bourbon and rye whiskey. One of the distinguishing features of American whiskey is the use of a mash bill – the recipe containing the desired, relative percentages of grains that will be brought together for the fermentation stage. In bourbon, the mash bill must contain a minimum of 51% corn; in rye, 51 % rye. The rest of the mash bill will contain at least a minimum of malted barley for the enzymes which convert starches to sugar. Wheat and rye in varying proportions are commonly used in the mash bill, but bourbons often exclude one of these.

Flow Chart: American Bourbon or Rye

Mash bill—>Milling grains separately—>Water—>Cooking of corn—>Add rye or wheat—>Add malted barley—>Adjust PH by adding Sour mash—>Add yeast—>Fermentation up to 3 days—>Produce beer , 5-6% ABV—>Distillation 1& condensation to approx. 55-60% ABV (acidic residue is sour mash for future use—>

Distillation 2

produces "white dog" at 80% ABV or less by law—>White dog reduced to 62.5%ABV or less—> cut point...>Maturation in new charred oak barrels—>Warehousing....>Bottling

After 1938, by law, all American whiskey had to be aged in new, charred barrels. The wood of choice has been American white oak (Quercus alba) with its distinctive gifts of flavor, as well as a strong, solid grain that resists leakage. In order to be a "straight" whiskey, as in the phrase Kentucky Straight Bourbon or Tennessee Straight Whiskey it has to be aged a minimum of 2 years and made in those respective states. Tennessee whiskey, like Jack Daniels, is basically a bourbon with one important difference. In Tennessee, the white dog is filtered through charcoal made from burned sugar-maple wood.

CANADIAN

I had no idea that Canadians went about making their whisky in a different way from distillers in the States, but then I didn't know anything about Canadian whisky until I began reading Davin de Kergommeaux. The United States and Canada trade grain with each other. Whisky ingredients crisscross the border to end up in both our whiskeys. The main difference between traditional American whiskey and Canadian whisky is that there is no mash bill for the latter. All the grains are separately made into whiskies, then brought together (married) for barreling and aging. It is a finessed spirit, if you will. The biggest producers may process all the grains in-house, but that isn't a requirement. Rye is heavily relied upon as a flavoring, added to a base whisky that is generally corn; however, barley and wheat are also components in some whiskies. Most Canadian whisky is considered "blended," and is often called "rye" even though it may not be in the American sense of the rye grain being at least 51% of the spirit.

Canadian is often considered milder, smoother and more delicate than rye whiskeys south of the border. My experience is that it is a lovely spirit. You'd think we'd drink more Canadian whisky! But walk into any liquor shop in the States and you'll find the Canadians under-represented. It is said that the Canadians tend to keep most of the better stuff on their side of the border. We can only hope that increasing interest and market demand will encourage Canadian distilleries to share more of their best whisky heritage with their southern neighbors

IRISH

Apologies to Irish whiskey-makers for brevity here. They make single malts from barley and they also make blended whiskey. A distinguishing feature of Irish whiskey is that most–but not all– involves triple distilling. Triple distilling contributes to a national flavor profile that is sweet and smooth.

JAPAN

While whisky production began in Japan as early as the 1870s, the first commercial whisky distillery was launched in 1924 in Yamazaki (Suntory) by Shinjiro Torii. He hired Masataka Taketsuru, who had studied distilling in Scotland, to head up the distillery. In 1934, Taketsuru left to form his own Yochi distillery in Hokkaido. This company would become Nikka. These are still the best- known companies in Japan. Japanese whisky-making would remain highly influenced by the Scots. Japanese whisky is noted for its harmony and balance. It is particularly crafted to accompany food. Japanese spirit's uniqueness (their terroir) also lies in the nature of their water, the innovative use and blending of multiple yeast types for fermentation, and finishing in Japanese (Mizunara) Oak

AROMA AND FLAVOR BY THE BARREL... AND CASK

It is true that whisky improves with age. The older I get, the more I like it.
–Ronnie Corbett.

We've noted that an amazing 60-80% of flavor arises from the aging and finishing process. Therefore, we need to understand something about the wood in which whiskey is aged.

Although experiments have been conducted using other woods, such as maple (Woodford Reserve) and Oregon "Garyanna" oak (Westland Distillery), American white oak (Quercus alba) has long been the preferred wood used in America, and in ex-bourbon barrels that are used world-wide. American oak has distinctive characteristics of density, durability, and the ability to hold fluid, particularly after charring, as well as to oxygenate the whiskey. American oak has lactones, tannins, sugars, and other properties that interact with esters and aldehydes to give whiskeys the aromas and flavors of vanilla, caramel, honey, nuts, baking spices, toast, coconut, butterscotch, coffee and mocha.

European oak (Quercus robur) grown in England and Scotland was traditionally used by whisky makers in Scotland and Ireland but, due to its slow growth and the tendency to produce twisted trunks, it was prone to inefficient cutting and leaks, so whisky makers switched to Russian oak for a time. But in the 1860s, whisky makers changed again after the popular importation of Spanish sherry. The sherry casks are made of Spanish oak. There are other sources of European oak, such as Hungary and other Eastern European countries, that are sometimes used for wine due to their resemblance to French oak.

French oak (Quercus robur) is widely used for wine maturation. Less common is the finer grained, Sessile oak (Quercus patraea or sessiliflora). Quercus patraea, grown in the Limousin forest is looser grained than the American white (alba) and yields less usable lumber. It costs twice that of American white oak. But Limousin, with more tannins, imparts complex flavors particularly suitable for Cognac, Armagnac, sherry and whiskey aging. Flavors include: dark chocolate, roasted coffee, toasted almond, and savory spices. It gives the spirit a silky texture.

Japanese Mizunara oak (Quercus mongolica) is rarely used, even in Japan. In that sense, it might be considered an elite finishing that bestows unique notes of terroir. Mizunara is soft, porous and prone to leaks. Therefore, it is mostly reserved for finishing. It imparts coconut, incense, smoky and pungent, and herbal flavor notes.

Just as Aprotosoaie, Luca and Miron reviewed the compounds contributing to chocolate aromas, K.-Y. Monica Lee and her colleagues in Scotland studied compounds that contribute to some perceived aromatics and flavors in order to revise a flavor wheel originally created by the Scottish Whisky Research Institute. These compounds arise at various stages of whisky production, including the maturation phrase. I am including some of what they reported, not to turn us all into food scientists, but to see that the link between these compounds and their sensory manifestations are specific and describable, and that fact holds out the potential for the future optimization of flavor development in whisky production.

FLAVOR WHEEL EQUIVALENT	COMPOUND
Pungent	Formic acid
Burnt smoky	Guaiacol
Medicinal	u-Cresol
Malty	Malted barley
	2- and 3- Methylbutanal
	4-Hydroxy-2(or 5)-ethyl-2(or 5)-methyl-3(2H) furanone 4
Grassy	Hexanal
Solventy	Ethylacetate
Fruity (Apple)	E-Icliyl hexanoate
Fruity (Banana, pear drop)	v»-Amyl acetate
Berry	Thiomenthone
Floral (Natural Rose, Violet)	Phenylethanol
Floral (Artificial)	Geraniol
Nutty (Coconut)	Whisky lactone
Marzipan	Furfural
Vanilla	Vanillin
Spicy	4-Vinyl guaiacol
Spicy (Clove)	Eugenol
Caramel	Maltol
Mothball	Naphthalene
Moldy	2.4,6-Ttrichloroanisole
Earthy, musty	Geosmin. 2-methyl «o-bomeol
Vinegary	Acetic acid
Cardboard	2-Nonenal

FLAVOR WHEEL EQUIVALENT	COMPOUND
Stagnant, rubbery	Dimethyl tri-sulphide (DMTS)
Yeasty	Hydrogen sulphide (H:S)
Rotten egg	Hydrogen sulphide
Meaty	Methyl (2-methyl-3-furyl) disulphides)
Vegetable	Dimethyl sulphide (DMS)
(Sweet Corn, Cooked Cabbage)	
Gassy	Ethanethiol
	3-Methyl-2-butene-l-thiol l28
Rancid	Butyric acid ethyl buryrate
Sweaty	iso-Valeric acid
Oily	Heptanol
Soapy	Ethyl laurate
	l-Decanol
Buttery	Diacetyl

8

THE AMAZING WORLD OF AROMA AND FLAVOR

Lose your mind and come to your senses.
— Frederick Salomon Perls

YOU HAVE NOW BEEN INTRODUCED TO the concept of flavor profiles. To be more precise, we are speaking of aroma and flavor. Even though seemingly experienced on the tongue and palate, beyond the basic taste perceptions of sweet, sour, bitter, salty and umami, other flavor notes actually reach sensory reception through the nasopharynx and the retro-nasal pathway. There, receptor cells detect chemical compounds and convert them into our body's neurotransmitters leading to the olfactory center of the brain. Associative memories then come into play.

Memory is often neglected in discussions of flavor. But think about it: if you've never tasted raspberries or apples, how would you be able to identify them? As a reviewer of chocolate, I've had to dedicate time to exploring fruits from regions in which I did not grow up. This has been the only way to construct a vocabulary of descriptors for communicating the complexity of what I was tasting. As a youngster growing up in New Jersey, I was not fortunate enough to taste some tropical produce, such as passion fruit. Pineapple, yes. But I didn't taste mango or papaya until I was in my late 20s. My early adult years in theatre and music took me mostly to New York and the British Isles. Therefore, as a middle-aged adult chocolate reviewer-in-training, I had to hunt down the rare produce markets that carried "exotic" fruits, then repeatedly exposed myself to their aromas and flavors in the hopes of getting them into my long-term memory and lexicon.

The wine, scotch and whiskey industries have long histories of studying, both perceptually and chemically, the aromas and flavors of their products. The chocolate industry has also studied flavor. But when most of those in the critical tasting and reviewing end of the chocolate world looked for ways to express subtle flavor experiences, they borrowed heavily from the sensory descriptors of the wine industry.

You can find graphic representations of flavor in the whiskey and chocolate industries in the form of flavor, or tasting, wheels. If you enter the search term "flavor wheel," you can pull up many examples. I include a few samples here of chocolate, single malt, and bourbon aroma and flavor wheels.

What can we do with aroma and flavor wheels? It helps us to search our memories for descriptors and put names to immediate sensory perceptions. We can taste new fruit, herbs, and spices, smell new flowers, locate and map these previously unfamiliar aromas and flavors onto a flavor wheel and thereby acquire new descriptors in our lexicon. We can then construct a check list of aromas and flavors from the descriptors found on the wheel, such as the inventories in this chapter. Then when we recognize these aromas and flavors we've stored in memory and check off the aromas and flavors we discover during a tasting of any particular chocolate or whiskey. We can determine which notes are in the nose or on the palate. We can describe each note we detect. Once we determine which flavors are dominant and minor, we can categorize the chocolate bar as reflecting a particular flavor profile, or possibly a composite, crossover profile.

We've already introduced the concept of using these flavor wheels and inventory check-lists in our How To Taste chapter. You can continue to use these templates for personal use when tasting any of the chocolates and whiskeys in the rest of this book.

CHOCOLATE AROMA AND FLAVOR WHEEL

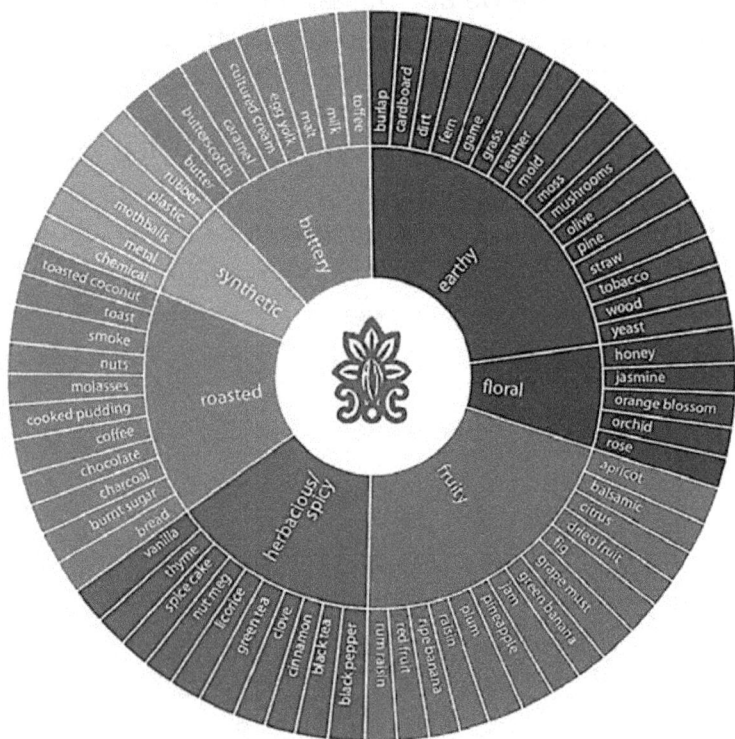

Inner ring: buttery, earthy, floral, fruity, herbacious/spicy, roasted, synthetic

Outer labels (clockwise from top):
burlap, cardboard, dirt, fern, game, grass, leather, mold, moss, mushrooms, olive, pine, straw, tobacco, wood, yeast, honey, jasmine, orange blossom, orchid, rose, apricot, balsamic, citrus, dried fruit, fig, grape must, green banana, jam, pineapple, plum, raisin, red fruit, ripe banana, rum raisin, black pepper, black tea, cinnamon, clove, green tea, licorice, nutmeg, spice cake, thyme, vanilla, bread, burnt sugar, charcoal, chocolate, coffee, cooked pudding, molasses, nuts, smoke, toast, toasted coconut, chemical, metal, mothballs, plastic, rubber, butter, butterscotch, caramel, cultured cream, egg yolk, malt, milk, toffee

CHOCOLATE AROMA/FLAVOR PROFILE INVENTORY

mark: a=aroma, f=flavor

FRUITY

Citrus: (pink) grapefruit—lemon—lime—orange—kumquat—blood orange—

Berry: blackberry—raspberry—strawberry—blackcurrant—blueberry—

Tree Fruit: dark cherry—tart cherry—apricot—peach—apple—pear—quince—

Dried Fruit: dark raisin—white raisin—currant—prune—mission fig—calimyrna fig—dates—apricot—jam—candied—

Fermented: balsamic—wine—yeast

Tropical : pineapple—banana—plantain—mango—papaya—sapote—passionfruit—lychee—guava

COMMENTS:

VEGETATIVE

Fresh: grass—eucalyptus—pine—mint—lemongrass—cilantro—

Cooked: asparagus—green olive—black olive

Dried: hay/straw—green tea—tobacco—

COMMENTS:

SUGAR/BUTTERY

milk—butter—cream—butterscotch—honey—brown sugar—caramel—molasses—

COMMENTS:

NUTTY

peanut—(toasted) almond—walnut—hazelnut—cashew—Brazil nut—pine nut—

COMMENTS:

SPICY/HERBAL

coffee—black tea—vanilla—cinnamon—black pepper—hot/red pepper—licorice—nutmeg—clove—allspice—star anise

COMMENTS

FLORAL

citrus/orange blossom—jasmine—violet—rose—orchid/vanilla—lavender—verbena—frangipani/plumeria—wild/raw honey—

COMMENTS:

CHOCOLATE AROMA/FLAVOR PROFILE INVENTORY

EARTHY
musky—soil—truffle—mushroom—forest decay—wood—mold—
cardboard—burlap—leather--nuts--tobacco--coffee--cocoa--black tea--
COMMENTS:

MISCELLANEOUS/BAKED/ROASTED/NAKED/BRUT

bread—toast—burnt sugar—espresso—mocha/moka—malt balls—co-
coa/"chocolatey"—
toasted coconut—roasted nut—naked/brut—umami–
COMMENTS:

CHEMICAL/OFF-NOTES
petroleum—tar—rubber—detergent—plastic—
metal—smoke—hammy—unripe—cheese—
COMMENTS:

CHOCOLATE FLAVOR PROFILES

After checking off descriptors on the Aroma/Flavor Profile Inventory, you can determine the dominant notes and see if they can be summarized as a Flavor Profile. Here are examples:

- Floral, Fruity
- Citrusy or Tropical Twang
- Earthy or Roasted or Nutty
- Spices & Herbs, Sugar & Buttery
- Naked or "Chocolatey," without nuance

Sometimes the descriptors don't fit neatly into just one of these profiles and are a crossover, composed of two or more profiles. Here are a few examples:

- Fruit & Floral (blackberry, sweet cherry & jasmine)
- Fruit (raspberry) & Roasted & Earthy (hazelnut, cocoa, woody) Fruit & Twang (berry & citrus)
- Earthy & Roasted (soil, cocoa & roast walnut) & Spice (cinnamon) Naked & whisper of Fruit
- Spice & Twang
- Sugar (Demerara) & Caramel & Roasted (hint of Nut)

If a crossover occurs, it's essential to determine exactly what those profile components are in order to successfully pair a chocolate with whiskey... or anything else. Sometimes even a hint of a flavor can prevent an optimal pairing. But if we can at least identify the dominant flavor notes and their profiles correctly, that will probably lead to an acceptable match within a range of possibilities. We can then tweak our selections. For example, let's say you want to match a chocolate bar with a crossover profile from our shopping list with a whiskey. Perhaps, you selected a bar, such as Green & Blacks 70%, that has a pre-dominantly Earthy profile, and some minor notes of Spice and Fruit. You will find that profile is broadly compatible within the North American rye or a high rye bourbon (more than 15% rye), the N3 category. That will narrow the range of possible pairings to a manageable search. Then you will need to find out which one of the whiskeys within the N3 category is most agreeable to your palate. You might try Crown Royal Northern Harvest Rye (a 90% rye) from the shopping list. If that is just an okay pairing, but doesn't quite please, you might try another N3, such as Bulleit Frontier Straight Kentucky Bourbon, a high rye (28%) or Woodford Reserve Distillers Select Kentucky Straight Bourbon with 18% rye. Of course, you can also start your pairing search with a whiskey you favor. Start with the flavor profile of the whiskey, this time, then find a matching profile in a chocolate.

SCOTCH AND SINGLE MALT FLAVOR PROFILES

Scotch single malt whisky flavor profiles of various brands and their specific expressions have been well studied and published by David Wishart, then expanded by the Selfbuilt Whisky Analysis website whiskeyanalysis.com. Dave Broom extended his analysis to world whiskeys, including Ireland and North America. In addition, Broom included blended whiskeys. Cyrille Mald and Alexandre Vingtier of France have also published on the flavor profiles of world whiskeys. I have borrowed heavily from these writers and built upon all the aforementioned works for this book and my evolving database. I still have a lot of work to do to pin down the profile notes in greater detail. Again, the more specific I can get in describing even minor flavor notes and classifying them, the more effective a match I can make pairing whiskey with chocolate or anything else.

Beginning with Scotch single malts, Wishart, a statistician, as well as whisky enthusiast, assigned letters to whiskies, from A to J to represent flavor profile cluster types. Selfbuilt reworked the Wishart data to describe super-cluster groups. So a whisky that might be an A for Wishart, might overlap to some extent with whiskies belonging to the B group or the C groups. Selfbuilt Whisky Analysis assigned those to the ABC super-cluster. Super-clusters may be thought of as paralleling the cross-over profiles of chocolates with all their subtleties and nuances. Dave Broom's categories are a bit broader, and his orientation was not statistical. But because his system included other world whiskeys, he expanded the potential use of flavor profiles.

BROOM FLAVOR PROFILES

SINGLE MALTS

M1: LIGHT & FRAGRANT, ROUGHLY EQUIVALENT TO WISHART G, H,
M2: FRESH & FRUITY, ROUGHLY EQUIVALENT TO WISHART E, F
M3: RICH & FRUITY, ROUGHLY EQUIVALENT TO WISHART A, B, C
M4: SMOKY, ROUGHLY EQUIVALENT TO WISHART I & J

BLENDS
B1: LIGHT & FRAGRANT B2: FRUITY & SPICY B:3 RICH & FRUITY B:4 SMOKY

There are many aroma, flavor, or tasting wheels for Scotch whisky. Aroma is most important to master-distillers and many go about their work mainly by nosing.

One of the most comprehensive wheels was created for The Scotch Research Institute (SWRI) by Drs. Jim Swan and Jennifer Newton in 1970. Decades later, Charles Maclean "reinvented the wheel" for Whisky Magazine and has since produced an updated version. While the Maclean wheel is a refinement from a perceptual or sensory point of view, in 2000 K. -Y. Monica Lee and her Scottish colleagues developed a revision of the original SWRI wheel combining hard science and sensory components.

.However, for our purposes, I like the wheel published by Westland Distillery for reasons stated in their product brochure. "One of the most challenging aspects of nosing and tasting is simply learning how to put a name to what you smell or taste. This tasting wheel was designed to help budding maltheads develop their 'aroma vocabulary.' Like the production of our whiskey, our version of the Tasting Wheel is informed by tradition but re-imagined for the American Single Malt Whiskey category. Gone are the charming but perplexing descriptors such as 'treacle' that you'll find in the U.K., for instance. Added are entirely new categories, such as Gourmand, which we've borrowed from the perfume industry. But the general approach remains the same: group flavor notes by family to deliver a quick and easy resource to help spark your memory."

The WESTLAND TASTING WHEEL

One of the most challenging aspects of nosing and tasting whiskey is simply learning how to put a name to what you smell or taste. This Tasting Wheel was designed to help budding maltheads develop their "aroma vocabulary". Like the production of our whiskey, our version of the Tasting Wheel is informed by tradition but re-imagined for the American Single Malt Whiskey category. Gone are the charming but perplexing descriptors such as "treacle" that you'll find in the U.K., for instance. Added are entirely new categories such as Gourmand, which we've borrowed from the perfume industry. But the general approach remains the same; group flavor notes by family to deliver a quick and easy resource to help spark your memory.

WESTLAND
DISTILLERY

2931 FIRST AVENUE SOUTH | SEATTLE, WA 98134
Telephone:(206) 787-7250
WWW.WESTLANDDISTILLERY.COM

Let's use the Westland Distillery Tasting Wheel to create a Single Malt Aroma & Flavor Inventory. You might notice that I've added a few descriptors to encompass Scottish, as well as American, single malts. All the notes added by R. M. Peluso are preceded by an asterisk(*). I've enclosed the word "feinty" in quotes as that is the term used on many Scottish flavor wheels. The feinty category includes aromas that are sulphury, oily, leathery, tobacco, sweaty, plastic, cheesy, and some that are honey-related. You will find feinty aromas appear under different headings on some wheels.

BARLEY-BASED SINGLE MALTS AND SCOTCH BLENDS AROMA & FLAVOR INVENTORY

mark: a=aroma, f=flavor

FRUITY
ARTIFICIAL: Bubble Gum—Fruit Pastry—Taffy Candy—Red Licorice
CITRUS: Lemon—Orange—Tangerine—Grapefruit—Lime
FRESH: Apple—Pear—Peach—*Nectarine—Banana—Pineapple—Melon
BERRIES: Raspberry—Strawberry—Cherry—Blackberry—Blueberry—Gooseberry—Pomegranate
DRIED: Prune—Raisin—Figs—Apricot—Plum—Mango—*Winey—(also see Gourmand)

FLORAL
EXOTIC: Orange Blossom—Carnation—Honeysuckle—Jasmine
GARDEN: Mint—Lavender—Sage—Rose—Rhododendron
WOODLAND: Green Leaves—Sandalwood—Fir Tree—Spruce—Cedar
FIELD: Barn—Tobacco Leaf—Grass—Hay—Heather

PEATY
SEA: Smoked Salmon—*Kippery—Oysters—Seaweed—Shellfish
EARTH: Moss—Bog—Turf—Forest Floor
SMOKY: Peet-Reek—Cigar—Incense—Campfire—*Barrel Char
MEDICINAL: Hospital—Iodine—Tar—Bandage

WOODY
MUSTY: Cloth—Pencils—Metallic—Cellar—Cardboard—Cork
TOASTY: Burnt—Aniseed—Coffee Grounds—Rice Pudding—Fennel
OILY: Waxy—Coconut—Suntan Oil—Butter—Almond Oil—Corn Oil
LUMBER: Sawdust—Sandalwood—Oaky—Resinous—Pine—*Other wood

*Off-notes (including "Feinty" & Sulphury)
VEGETATIVE: Cooked Corn—Cabbage—Peas—Cooked Carrots—Pop corn
CHEESY/MEATY: Pot roast—Burnt Steak—Fishy—Burnt Milk—*Cheesy--Rotten Eggs
RUBBER: Rubber Tires—New Shoes—Burnt Rubber—Pencil Eraser
BURNT: Fireworks—Struck Matches—Gun Powder
*CHEMICAL/OTHER: Nail polish remover—Solvent—Plastic—Leather—Sweaty

Grainy & *Roast
DOUGH: Flour—Grist—Biscuit—Scone—Pancake—Croissant—
SWEET GRAIN: Cinnamon Roll—Cookies—Waffle Cone—Shortcake—Graham Cracker
BAKED: Pie—Crumble—Waffle—Pound Cake—Fruit Cake—Muffin—
BREAD & *CEREAL: Multigrain—Wheat—Rye—Sourdough—Toast—*Oat—Malt—
NUTS: Hazelnut—Pecan—Almonds—*Toasted almond—Peanut—Pistacchio—Walnut

NORTH AMERICAN BOURBON AND RYE

Many flavor wheels exist for bourbon and rye separately, such as the Woodford Reserve Bourbon Flavor Wheel, reprinted below. However, I like the Bourbon and Banter wheel, also reprinted here, because it recognizes, and creates a space to express, the relative proportions of various grains that may make up mash bills (USA) and blends of grains (Canada).

BOURBON & BANTER
est. 2011
DRINK CURIOUS

BOURBON FLAVOR WHEEL

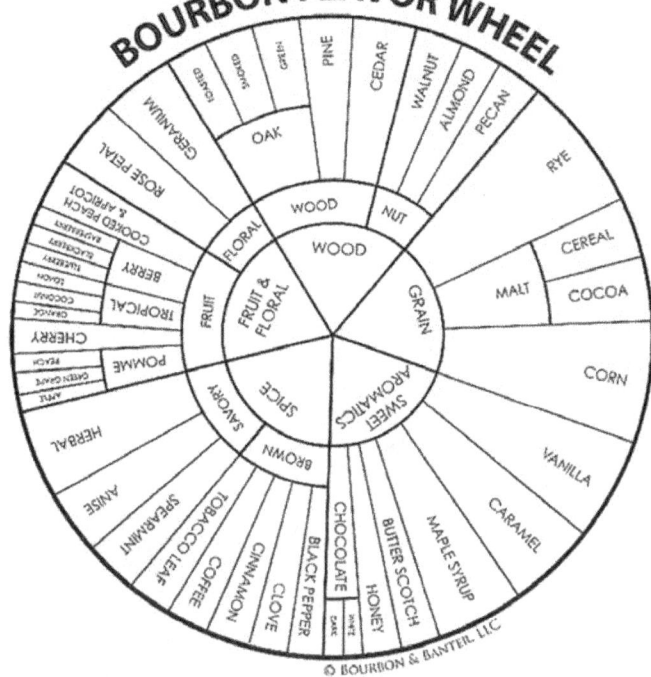

© BOURBON & BANTER LLC

Help spread the bourbon gospel online – BourbonBanter.com • @BourbonBanter •

Facebook.com/BourbonBanter

BOURBON & RYE WHISKEY
AROMA & FLAVOR INVENTORY

AROMA = A   FLAVOR = F

GRAIN
CORN – RYE –
MALT: CEREAL–COCOA–

SWEET AROMATICS
VANILLA–
CARAMEL–
MAPLE SYRUP–
BUTTERSCOTCH–
HONEY–
MARZIPAN–
CHOCOLATE: DARK–WHITE–

WOOD
OAK: GREEN–SMOKED–TOASTED–
CHAR–
PINE–
CEDAR–
NUT: WALNUT– ALMOND– PECAN–

FRUIT
GREEN APPLE–
APPLE–
PEACH–
CHERRY–
ORANGE– LEMON–
COCONUT–
BERRY: BLACKBERRY–BLUEBERRY–RASPBERRY–
COOKED: PEACH–APRICOT–
DRIED: APRICOT–

FLORAL
ROSE PETAL–
HONEYSUCKLE–

SPICES & HERBS
BLACK PEPPER–
CLOVE–
NUTMEG–
CARDAMOM–
CINNAMON–
COFFEE–
TOBACCO LEAF–
MINT–
ANISE–
OTHER HERBAL–

In addition to classifying single malts and blends, Dave Broom has attempted to describe the flavor profiles of North American whiskeys. In Whiskey, The Manual, he omitted the Rich and Oaky category found in his book The World Atlas of Whisky; I've found it helpful to reintroduce that here. In addition, within the North American bourbon category, I found Fred Minnick's discussion of salient, or "forward" flavors also insightful: whenever possible, I've incorporated Minnick's descriptors.

Broom Flavor Profiles

North American Whiskeys
NAM-1 Corn Fed (bourbon, corn whiskey)
NAM-2 Sweet Wheat
NAM-3 High Rye

Broom also described a Rich & Oaky category in The World Atlas of Whisky

Peluso Modifications and Additions
N 1=Broom
NAM1=soft corn dominant bourbon or corn whiskey
N2=Broom
NAM 2= high wheat bourbon or wheat whiskey
N 3=Broom
NAM 3= rye whiskey
N1/3=high rye bourbon
N1/R&O= corn dominant Rich & Oaky
N2/R&O=sweet wheat Rich & Oaky
N-B=North American Single Malt (barley-based)
N-B/P=North American Peated Single Malt
N-B/S=North American Single Malt Sherry Cask Finished
N-1/P= Peated bourbon

Minnick's Salient Flavors in Bourbon (Peluso Notation)
Grain Forward (g)
Nutmeg Forward (n)
Caramel Forward (c)
Cinnamon Forward (ci)

9

PAIRING BY FLAVOR PROFILES

I have struggled happily with similar combinations and have discovered many wonderful flavor surprises...
—*John Scharffenberger,*

THE DATA UPON WHICH I've based this book, is still evolving, intentionally. As new chocolates are created, as whiskeys debut in the marketplace, or as I simply add ones I didn't get to previously, they can be added to the database. After collecting information on over 100 chocolate bars and more than 70 whiskeys, patterns began to stand out. There are some profiles of both chocolate and whiskey which are more versatile and more easily matched. Conversely, some whiskeys and chocolates are quirkier and will take a refined search. As I was collecting the data, I made note of the dominant flavors constituting the profiles, but also the more idiosyncratic notes that may stand out as a variation on the broader flavor profile class. An optimal match must take all of that into consideration.

Having discussed the flavor profiles for chocolate and whiskey, let's explore that which, based on my evolving database, generally works in pairing. The question I asked myself while reviewing the data was "which paired chocolate and whiskey profiles work optimally?" On a rating scale of 1 to 10, only those matches ranking 7 or above made the final cut. So the results as reported in these pages reflect that high standard. Initially, I will present, in broad terms, those chocolate and whiskey profiles most likely to result in a compatible pairing. Keep in mind that both chocolates and whiskeys are nuanced. Remember the terms Cross Over (chocolate profiles) and Super Cluster (whisky profiles), that means we have to introduce more precision by describing the areas of congruence for overlapping flavor profiles. A minor flavor note can open up a possibility not seen in a generalization about pairing any particular profiles as presented in this chapter. We can probably find members of any profile category that will surprise us by pairing well, even though, at first glance, they appear as low-probability mates, simply because we didn't account for every flavor nuance. In the next chapters, you will find more specific examples of pairings, with some exceptional or quirkier notes that make possible matches with less likely partners. As those specific cases arise, I will point out the unique, minor flavor notes that might make those less likely matches possible.

Some general principles became apparent as I went about testing candidate pairs: The most sensually pleasing combinations involved bars with a smoother consistency and tended to be higher in percentage of cacao butter content. Chocolate that coated the tongue in a uniform manner and melted evenly worked much better with whiskey than grainy (rustic style) or drier bars. Brut bars with cacao content 80% or higher were more challenging matches. Optimal candidates for whiskey pairings were chocolate bars with 75% cacao or below. The well-established "sweet spot" of the 70% cacao content chocolate bars proved itself to stand up particularly well with whiskey. Can exceptions to these parameters make for successful pairings? Sure.I include a few in these pages. It's just less likely.

CHOCOLATE FLAVOR PROFILE	WHISKEY FLAVOR PROFILE
MOST VERSATILE	**MOST FREQUENTLY COMPATIBLE WITH**
Fruity/ Fruit & Floral Fr/FF	Wishart Single Malt type A: full-bodied sherried, fruity, honey & spice Broom type NAM 3 (N3, N-1/3Peluso): rye/high rye bourbon Second Most Compatible With Wishart Single Malt type E: medium-bodied, medium-sweet, fruity, honey, malty, winey, some smoke Wishart Single Malt type G: light-bodied, sweet, honey, floral, fruity, spicy Broom type NAM 1 (N1, Peluso): classic bourbon
Earthy E	Most Frequently Compatible With Wishart Single Malt type G: light-bodied, sweet, honey, floral, fruity, spicy Wishart Single Malt type E: medium-bodied, medium-sweet, fruity, honey, malty, winey, some smoke Broom types NAM1, NAM2, NAM3 (Peluso N1, N2, N3): classic bourbon, high wheat, high rye
Naked ("Chocolatey") N	Most Frequently Compatible With Wishart Single Malt type G: light-bodied, sweet, honey, floral, fruity, spicy Wishart Single Malt type A: full-bodied sherried, fruity, honey & spice Second Most Compatible With Broom type NAM 2 (N2, Peluso) high wheat bourbon or wheat whiskey
Less Versatile	Most Frequently Compatible With
Twang T	Wishart Single Malt type E: medium-bodied, medium-sweet, fruity, honey, malty, winey, some smoke Broom types NAM1, NAM2, NAM3 (Peluso N1, N2, N3): classic bourbon, high wheat, high rye
Spices & Herbs S&H dark (not dark milk)	Most Frequently Compatible With Wishart Single Malt types I&J: Second Most Compatible With Wishart Single Malt type E: medium-bodied, medium-sweet, fruity, honey, malty, winey, some smoke

10

AH! THE PEAT. MATCHING CHOCOLATE TO PEATY SINGLE MALTS

"I sipped my scotch. It was smoky and smooth, tasting of peat and aged oak, underscored by licorice and the intangible essence of Scottish masculinity. I liked my scotch undiluted, like I liked my truth."
— *Viet Thanh Nguyen*

WHEN I WAS IN MY LATE TEENS, I took a train across the Scottish highlands. All these years later, I still recall miles of countryside, herds of sheep, stone fences and isolated farmhouses, rolling hills, vast expanses of moors, and heather growing everywhere. Whenever I smell peated whisky, I'm back on that train, fogging up the window as I silently mouth "wow" too close to the glass.

Love it or hate it, peated whisky is an acquired taste for many. Mention peat, and smoke comes to mind. But all smoke is not created equal. Personally, I don't care for the heavy, charred maple smoke in Tennessee whiskey (you may love it!), but I took to peaty smoke right away. I find it rich and evocative of place. And isn't that what terroir is all about? Some peated whiskies from the Hebrides carry you to the sea, the smell of fish or seaweed. Other peated whiskies serve up the floral notes of heather. Thousands of years cut up and fed to kilns ends up in your glass.

Degree of peating is measured in phenol parts per million, or PPM, in the lab. While, theoretically, it suggests how heavy the peat flavor is, it's not quite that simple. There are many components that constitute our final perception of peat. I've personally tasted some supposedly heavily peated whiskies only to experience them as rather mild. Laphroaig and Lagavulin are regarded as "peat monsters," and deservedly so, however, I would not have guessed Westland exceeded them in PPM. I would have also been in error judging Port Charlotte as less peaty than Laphroaig. As you go about trying these whiskies, see what you think.

SOME PUBLISHED PPMS FOR SEVERAL WELL- KNOWN WHISKIES

- Kings County Peated Bourbon: 15-25 ppm
- Connemara 12 year: 20 ppm
- Highland Park -20 ppm
- Lagavulin - 35 ppm
- Laphroaig - 40 ppm
- Bruichladdich Port Charlotte: 40 ppm
- Westland American Peated Single Malt: 55 ppm
- Bruichladdich, Octomore: 167-169ppm

SCOTLAND'S PEATY SINGLE M ALTS

Let's start with a couple Scottish classics from Islay island. These are well known enough to find at an upscale local bar. But I must warn you, I once took some Laphroaig 10 home in a flask, and no matter what I did, I couldn't get the aroma out. It was like the parking valet's body odor in Seinfeld's car (find it on YouTube!), only not unpleasant. Still, I wanted the odor out so I could use the container when absconding with other whiskeys. No luck. I tried washing it in vinegar, in baking soda, gallons and gallons of hot sudsy water. Nothing worked. Nothing! There was only one thing to do—the flask has now become my dedicated Islay take-home carrier. Strong peat with marine characteristics—goes right in that flask.

While some brands from the islands are downright fishy, Lagavulin 16 and Laprhoaig 10 are more salt air, seaweed, and medicinal notes. But combine them with the wrong chocolate, and you get a medicine cabinet. These whiskies fit the Wishart J profile: full-bodied, dry, very smoky, and pungent. And they tend to match chocolates with a Citrusy Twang or a Spice & Herb profile. These whiskies can tolerate chocolates with higher cacao content, such as an 80% (brut). Also from Islay, is Bruichladdich's Port Charlotte Scottish Barley (I). The profile is medium dry, medium sweet, moderate smoke, and no medicinal notes. Personally, I like the Bruichladdich expressions a lot. Both the Port Charlotte and Octomore lines are heavily peated. Octomore is higher in price, but certainly worth traveling across town to try at a tasting.

Highland Park is one of Scotland's most respected brands from its northernmost island, Orkney, a place heavily influenced by Norse culture. In fact, Highland Park is Scotland's northern-most distillery. HP's whisky is known for combining sherry cask aging with peat. You'll find fruit along with smoke and lovely heather notes. The third chocolate profile frequently compatible with peated whiskey, more often with the I group, is a crossover profile of Earth & Fruit—you can particularly see that in the Irish Connemara pairings. A fruit profile—not a citrusy fruit which seems able to stand up to I

DEEP TASTING CHOCOLATE & WHISKEY

& J on its own– requires earthy elements or naked "chocolatey" backbone to work with these peated whiskies, and that extends to the peated whiskeys of America that use Scottish peat. I have not yet included peated whisky from other countries, such as India, but I would predict that they would follow the same pattern.

Whisky flavor profiles appear in parenthesis.

BEST MATES WITH LAGAVULIN 16 YEAR SINGLE MALT (J)

The Lagavulin Distillery (at Kildalton) dates back to 1816 officially, but they were engaged in illicit whisky-making as early as 1742. Renamed Lagavulin in 1817, they are now a subsidiary of Diageo. diageo.com

Nose: Smoke, smoke, and more smoke, peat, brine, iodine, umami, whisper of sherry and berries
Palate: rich, malty, dry, peat, seaweed, sherry flash, tobacco, and oak.
Finish: Long, spicy, peat smoke, oak, black pepper

Marou Faiseurs de Chocolat (Vietnam), Tien Giang 80%:
Profile: S&H
Subdues nutty notes and adds citrusy tartness to this chocolate's spice and herb profile.
marouchocolate.com

French Broad (USA), Costa Rica 80%
Profile: E&Fr
frenchbroadchocolates.com

Fresco (USA), San Martin, Peru 70% Profile: S&H
frescochocolate.com

BEST MATES WITH LAPHROAIG 10 (J)

Founded by The Johnstons in 1815, the distillery remained in the family for 139 years. The history is fascinating—all those wars with the neighbors—so I encourage you to visit laphroaig.com to read more. Laphroaig appears to be one of the few independent distilleries and has its own malting floor.
Nose: Peat smoke, bandaids (yep, not the only one to catch that whiff—but don't be turned off) seaweed, salt water, vanilla, oak.
Palate: Dry, peaty, smoky, salt, medicinal, malt, citrus zest and pepper
Finish: long, smoky, medicinal

BONNAT (FRANCE), MADAGASCAR 75%. PROFILE: T

Umami notes in this batch by Bonnat. Works amazingly well. Trails mint.
bonnat-chocolatier.com

RITUAL CHOC OLATE (USA), BALAO , ECUADOR 75% PROFILE: E& S

A minty finish shows up here too.
ritualchocolate.com

MAROU FAISEURS DE CHOCOLAT (VIETNAM) TIEN GIANG 70 %

Profile: S& H
The third to stage a minty exit in combination with the whisky.
marouchocolate.com

HOJA VERDE (ECUADOR) 66% PROFILE : F & S

Vanilla! Although there is no vanilla in the chocolate.
hojaverdechocolate.com

A MATE FOR BRUICHLADDICH 'S PORT CHARLOTTE SCOTTISH BARLEY (I)

Nose: ocean perfume, peat smoke, charred oak, iodine, leather, tobacco, vanilla, figs and dates, malt, nut

Palate: smoky malt, ocean, vanilla, toffee, hint of citrus, oak
Finish: long

AKESSON 'S (UK) BEJOFO ESTATE , MADAGASCAR , CRIOLLO 75%
Profile: T& Fr (berry)
akessons-organic.com

BEST MATES FOR HIGHLAND PARK 12 YEAR (I)
Nose: Heather, honey, peat smoke
Palate: Smoky, hints of dark chocolate, honey, orange zest and cinnamon
Finish: Long, smoky, citrus and chocolate whispers

SOMA CHOCOLATE MAKER (CANADA), CSB CHAMA, VZ 70%,
Profile: N &Fr
somachocolate.com

PATRIC CHOCOLATE (USA) MADAGASCAR 67% PROFILE: T
Emphasizes malt
patric-chocolate.com

IRELAND

It is said that Irish monks brought distilled spirit to Scotland sometime after the late 12th Century. Jameson, a Scot, returned the favor centuries later. Peated whiskey used to be common in Ireland along with other whiskeys. In fact, Ireland had a great variety of whiskeys, celebrated for the smoothness attributed to their iconic triple distilling process. There used to be hundreds of distilleries in Ireland. But the whiskey industry was hammered almost into extinction in the early 20th century, due to the Irish war of independence, American prohibition, and the world-wide Great Depression. The world wars didn't help either. Also, shifting tastes were a big factor. From over 37 in Dublin alone in the 1890s, only 3 large distilleries were left standing in all of Ireland before Harvard-educated John Teeling returned to his native country to become the father of the Irish whiskey renaissance. Teeling founded Cooley Distilling Company in the late 1980s. The good news is that Irish spirits have come roaring back and are now considered the fastest-growing spirit in the world. (I think that assertion underestimates the momentum of the American craft whiskey movement, but...) Connemara by Kilbeggan Distilling Company, launched under Teeling, was the first peated whiskey to return to Ireland. Today, Beam Suntory is the owner.

BEST MATES FOR CONNEMARA, PEATED SINGLE MALT, IRISH WHISKEY (I)
Nose: Peat smoke, malt, floral, honey
Palate: Smooth, peat, malt, sweet
Finish: Long, honey, peat smoke
kilbeggandistillingcompany.com

WOODBLOCK (USA), CAJAMARCA, PERU 70% PROFILE: E& FR
Muscular combination which enriches the peat.
woodblockchocolate.com

SOL CACAO, ECUADOR, (ORO VERDE) CEDEÑO FARMS 70 %
Profile: E& T
This bar amplifies and opens up the peat.
solcacao.com

AMERICAN PEAT?

Yes! Entrepreneurial craft distillers have been producing peated whiskey, as barley-based single malts, as is the case of Westland Distillery of Seattle, Washington. Craft distillers are doing exciting things in America. As far as I have been able to discern, most of the peat used in the States has been sourced from Scotland. But things are changing at Westland Distillery which recently created a peated single malt using local, Washington State peat. Instead of heather and Scottish vegetation, according to an interview Master Distiller Matt Hoffman recently gave to Whisky Advocate magazine, the Washington State peat contains cranberry, mint and other herbs, including a plant called Labrador tea, that is a traditional component of native American tea remedies. The plant is aromatic, oozing notes of rosemary, lavender and citrus when crushed. As a Westland fan, I was disappointed to learn that I'll have to wait three more years to taste that whiskey. Ah, well! You can't rush good whiskey. But I'm checking off the days on my calendar. Read more about Westland Distillery in the next chapter on single malts.

Americans, seldom missing an opportunity to innovate, have also launched some odd fellows. In Brooklyn, Kings County Distillery has created a peated bourbon. I like it! In Kings County Peated Bourbon, the peat is almost whispered. And as a bourbon, it's in a category all of its own. Well, almost. Corsair has produced a Triple Smoke Small Batch Bourbon, but I've yet to try it. So, sorry, no report. Other distillers will surely jump in. However, the Kings County is a gentle way for bourbon lovers to wade into peated spirit. This whiskey does a pleasing job of turning up the volume on the flavors of its chocolate pairing partners.

BEST MATES FOR WESTLAND AMERICAN PEATED SINGLE MALT (N-B/P)
Nose: Peat smoke, orange zest, baking spices, barley malt
Palate: Earthy and herbal, peat, coffee, vanilla, dried fruit
Finish: Cinnamon, smoke
westlanddistillery.com

SOMA CHOCOLATE MAKER (CA), CSB CHAMA, VZ 70% PROFILE: N &FR
Soma's bar adds body and richness to this peated whiskey.
somachocolate.com

CASTRONOVO CHOCOLATE (USA), AMAZONAS, VZ 70% PROFILE: N
castronovochocolate.com

CASTRONOVO CHOCOLATE, SIERRA NEVADA, COLUMBIA 72%
Profile: Fr & S
Castronovo's offering boosts the peat and adds fuller body to the
whiskey. Not for everyone!

BEST MATES FOR KINGS COUNTY PEATED BOURBON (N1/P)
Nose: Mildest peat smoke, sweet corn, whisper of orange zest,
vanilla, oak, shoe polish
Palate: Hints of chocolate, forward lime notes, leather and peat
Finish: Caramel, back to orange zest, white pepper, exits beerish
kingscountydistillery.com

DANDELION (USA), ZORZAL, DOMINICAN REPUBLIC, 70%
Profile: Earthy tobacco, berry, trails raw walnut.
dandelionchocolate.com

CREO (USA), HACIENDA LIMÓN, HEIRLOOM, ECUADOR 73%
Profile: Earthy cocoa, nut, caramel & red fruit.
This pairing gives depth to both partners.
creochocolate.com

PRALUS (FRANCE), MADAGASCAR 75%
Profile: T & Fr (berry)
Grapefruit zest. Red fruit becomes more intensely red and trails
off zest.
chocolats-pralus.com

AKESSON'S (UK) BEJOFO ESTATE, MADAGASCAR, CRIOLLO 75%
Profile: T& Fr (berry)
Becomes nuttier, zestier, but pleasantly so.
akessons-organic.com

11

LUSCIOUS PAIRINGS: CHOCOLATE AND OTHER SINGLE MALTS

There is no bad whiskey. There are only some whiskeys that aren't as good as others.
–Raymond Chandler

BRENNE SINGLE MALT WHISKY (FRANCE)

ON ONE OF MY MANY liquor store tasting forays, I had the privilege of meeting Allison Parc, a former dancer who fell in love with whisky. After researching her passion, she found the business opportunity she had been looking for on a farm in the Cognac region of France. Brenne's signature French single malt whisky is made with French barley, then aged 6-8 years in French (Limousin) oak. The pièce de résistance: Allison inspired her French partner to finish the whisky in ex-cognac casks. As much Cognac terroir as you can get! drinkbrenne.com

119

BEST MATES FOR BRENNE (M1, GH)

Delicate, floral, fruity (apple, banana liquor) vanilla and creme brûlée notes give this whisky amazing versatility with chocolate

MAROU FAISEURS DE CHOCOLAT (VIETNAM), DONG NAI, 72%

Profile: E, S & COCOA & NUT

Brenne warms the flavors and pushes them from creme brûlée to bread pudding.

MAROU FAISEURS DE CHOCOLAT (VIETNAM), TIEN GIANG 70%

Profile: S&H

This combination turns up the creme brûlée.

marouchocolate.com

MAP CHOCOLATE (USA), (I DREAM OF) FIJI 78%

Profile: FL & N

More flavor dimensions emerge as a duo: lighter fruit (sultanas) and cinnamon.

mapchocolate.com

CASTRONOVO CHOCOLATE (USA), HONDURAS, THE LOST CITY, 70%,

Profile: E

Raspberry puts in an appearance.

castronovochocolate.com

BAR AU CHOCOLATE (USA), SAMBIRANO, MADAGASCAR, 70 %

Profile: FR &T

Finishes distinctly cherry.

barauchocolat.com

BAR AU CHOCOLATE (USA), DUARTE PROVINCE, DOMINICAN REPUBLIC, 70%

Profile: FR &FL

barauchocolat.com

BAR AU CHOCOLATE (USA) COSTA RICA 72%
Profile: Earthy, coffee, grain, hint of berry.
barauchocolat.com

EXCELLENT COMBINATIONS!

AMEDEI (ITALY) 9, 75%
Profile: E&FF
Turns up the nut, mocha and caramel.
amedei.com

FRENCH BROAD CHOCOLATES (USA) NORINDINO, PERU 70%
Profile: T
Turns up the cognac!
frenchbroadchocolates.com

TEELING, THE SPIRIT OF DUBLIN, IRELAND
Teeling calls itself "The Spirit of Dublin–A Craft Revival." And revival it is, indeed. The original distillery, established in 1782 by patriarch, Walter Teeling, in the Liberties area of Dublin, is long gone. But a lot of history has washed down the Liffey since. Irish whiskey suffered a calamitous decline due to events, such as the Irish War of Independence 1919-21, American Prohibition 1920-33, and the Great Depression. The Emerald Isle's entire population of whiskey distilleries swooned to just 3 by the late 20th century, and Dublin's last one closed in 1976.
Enter the current generation of Teelings—Stephen and Jack, sons of John Teeling, considered to be the father of the Irish whiskey renaissance and the founder of Cooley Distillery (1987). Stephen and Jack brought whiskey-making back to the Liberties area of Dublin with the first new distillery in 125 years.

Whisky flavor Profiles appear in parenthesis.

BEST MATES FOR TEELING, SMALL BATCH IRISH WHISKEY (IRELAND) (E)
Finishing 6 months in rum casks renders this whiskey sweet and smooth.
Nose: Floral, honey and tree fruit notes
Palate: Baked apple on the palate accompanied by baking spices, and creamy vanilla
Finish: Herbal and caramel
teelingwhiskey.com

MAROU FAISEURS DE CHOCOLAT (VIETNAM) BA RIA 76%
Pops carob and peanut

MAROU FAISEURS DE CHOCOLAT TIEN GIANG 70%
Profile: S & H
Turns up creme brûlée.
marouchocolate.com

PUMP STREET BAKERY (UK) GRENADA, 70%
Profile: FF
pumpstreetbakery.com

SOMA CHOCOLATE MAKER (CANADA) BLACK SCIENCE, OCUMARE, VZ 70%
Profile: Fr&E
Cherry beckons.
somachocolate.com

LETTERPRESS CHOCOLATE (USA), UCAYALI, ECUADOR, 70%
Profile: S&H&Fr
Excellent!
letterpresschocolate.com

Askinosie CHOCOLATE (USA), MABABU, TANZANIA 72%
Profile: Fr&E
Pops black currant.
askinosie.com

THE DALMORE DISTILLERY OF THE SCOTTISH HIGHLANDS
On the shores of the North Sea-windswept Cromarty Firth, Alexander Matheson founded The Dalmore in 1839. Sold to Andrew and Charles Mackenzie in 1867, they introduced the Royal Stagg emblem that graces every bottle and the myth, tradition, and culture that has been the legacy of The Dalmore ever since. This distillery's artistry lies in its unique stills and its innovative aging processes. Whiskies are matured in American white oak from the Ozarks, and casks sourced for over a hundred years from the same sherry producer (Gonzalez Byass). After laying down the basic flavors from both, the various expressions of The Dalmore are subject to further finishing in casks that once contained Cabernet Sauvignon, Madeira, Marsala, or Port, each imparting distinct fruit notes. Every one of their whiskies are a privilege to savor. Our introduction is the Dalmore 12 Year.
thedalmore.com

BEST MATES FOR DALMORE 12 YEAR (SCOTLAND) (E)
Nose: Citrus, chocolate, spices
Palate: Oloroso sherry, orange, marzipan, vanilla
Finish: Roasted coffee and chocolate

PATRIC CHOCOLATE (USA) MADAGASCAR 67%
Profile: T
patric-chocolate.com

MAROU FAISEURS DE CHOCOLAT (VIETNAM) LAM DONG 74%
Profile: N&FF&S
A classy experience!
marouchocolate.com

MAROU FAISEURS DE CHOCOLAT(VIETNAM) TIEN GIANG 70%
Profile: S&H
marouchocolate.com

BAR AU CHOCOLAT (USA), DUARTE PROVINCE, DOMINICAN REPUBLIC 70%
Profile: FF
Pops rum and cherry.
barauchocolat.com

EXCELLENT COMPANIONS

SOMA (CANADA) BLACK SCIENCE, OCUMARE, VZ, 70%
Profile: Fr & E
The Dalmore really opens up the fruit.
somachocolate.com

LETTERPRESS (USA) UCAYALI 70%
Profile: S&H&Fr
Turns rich and oaky. The harmonious body tames some of the fruit acids.
letterpresschocolate.com

PUMP STREET BAKERY (UK) GRENADA 70%
Profile: FF
Hmm. Where'd that strawberry come from?
pumpstreetbakery.com

BONNAT (FRANCE) XOCUNUSCO, MEXICO 75%
Profile: N
Brings forward brandy and caramel.
bonnat-chocolatier.com

BRUICHLADDICH OF ISLAY ISLE, SCOTLAND
Pronounced "Broochkladdie" from the isle of "eyelah," but no matter how you say it, the entire Bruichladdich line, from non-peated to heavily peated, is a love letter to the world from the Hebrides. Theirs is a complex aging and finishing process utilizing a series of cask types. Personally, I've never sipped a disappointing dram from any of the Bruichladdich lines (including, Port Charlotte, Octomore, and Black Art) which produces value at any price point.
bruichladdich.com

BEST MATES FOR BRUICHLADDICH CLASSIC LADDIE (SCOTLAND) (G)
Nose: Barley sugar, mint, wild flowers, marine notes, caramel, fruits, candied citrus and honey
Palate: Oak, barley, apple, brown sugar, cinnamon and sweet malt.
Finish: Malt, toffee, honey.

MAROU FAISEURS DE CHOCOLAT (VIETNAM), TIEN GIANG 80%
Profile: S & H
Simply excellent duo! Better than with Marou Ba Ria, although the latter really pops the fruit.
marouchocolate.com

PUMP STREET BAKERY (UK), GRENADA, 70% PROFILE: FF
pumpstreetbakery.com

SOMA CHOCOLATE MAKER (CANADA) CBS CHAMA, 70%
Profile: Fr & E
somachocolate.com

EXCELLENT COMPANIONS

FRENCH BROAD (USA), COSTA RICA 80% PROFILE: E & FR
Turns brandyish.
frenchbroadchocolates.com

ORIGINAL BEANS (NETHERLANDS), WILD BENI, 66%
Profile: FF & honey
The Laddie inspires peanut, ginger ale, cereal and fudge notes to emerge.
originalbeans.com

BAR AU CHOCOLAT (USA), SAMBIRANO VALLEY, MADAGASCAR 70%
Profile: Fr&T
Spins out cognac.
barauchocolat.com

BEST MATES FOR BRUICHLADDICH ISLAY BARLEY 2009 (J)
While Bruichladdich uses only Scottish barley, this expression uses only the grain grown on Islay.
Nose: Fruity aromas may include :gooseberries, apple, pineapple, mango, apple, grapes, peach, plum, dates; floral, mint, bourbon and vanilla, oak, oloroso sherry.
Palate: Malty, honey, citrus, almonds, toffee apple, banana, ginger biscuits, sherry, oak, barley.
Finish: Cereal

FRUITION (USA) HEIRLOOM COSTA RICA 74% PROFILE: T
tastefruition.com

LETTERPRESS CHOCOLATE (USA) UCAYALI 70% PROFILE: S&H&FR
Adds smoke and dimension.
letterpresschocolate.com

GLENLIVET 12 YEAR (SCOTLAND) (E)

Located in Speyside's Livet Valley, Glenlivet was founded by George Smith who was granted the first legal license to distill in 1824. The Glenlivet 12 is aged in American ex-bourbon and European oak. Their special water source is "Josie's Well." Glenlivet is part of Malt Whisky Distilleries.

Nose: Light floral, tropical fruits, apple, honey, spice, hint of smoke
Palate: Medium body, sweet, smooth, pineapple, floral, honey, vanilla
Finish: Long, creamy, marzipan, apple, ginger, sherry.

Read about the smugglers' trail and excisemen at
maltwhiskydistilleries.com.

FRESCO ARTISAN CHOCOLATE (USA), SAN MARTIN, PERU 70%

Profile: S&H
The spice and fruit shine.
frescochocolate.com

LETTERPRESS (USA) UCAYLI, PERU 70% Profile: S&H&Fr

All three of these Letterpress offerings, given their Earth and Fruit notes, work well with the oak, vanilla, tree fruit and gingery malt of the Glenlivet 12. letterpresschocolate.com

LETTERPRESS (USA) ESMERALDAS, ECUADOR, 70%

Profile: E&Honey&Fr
letterpresschocolate.com

LETTERPRESS (USA) BELIZE, 70% Profile: E&Fr&S

letterpresschocolate.com

SCHARFFENBERGER (USA) EXTRA RICH MILK 41%
Profile: E & nut (almond) &caramel
Rich and rewarding. Body is added to both chocolate and the
whisky. Smoke note stoked, ginger tamed.
scharffenberger.com

BALVENIE 12 YEAR DOUBLEWOOD (SCOTLAND) (A)
Balvenie is a Speyside distillery built by William Grant in 1892
and is a subsidiary of William Grant & Sons, Ltd. The 12 year
Doublewood has been aged first in American ex-bourbon oak,
then Spanish oak, ex-Oloroso sherry casks for an additional nine
months, followed by whiskies married in oak for 3-4 months.
Nose: Sweet, fruity, Oloroso sherry, honey,vanilla.
Palate: Smooth, sweet, nutty, cinnamon, sherry.
Finish: Long
thebalvenie.com

SOMA (CANADA), CSB CHAMA, VZ, 70%
Profile: N&Fr
So good, I dropped my mouse!
somachocolate.com

PUMP STREET (UK), GRENADA, 70%
Profile: FF
Accents creaminess, creates great texture together.
pumpstreetbakery.com

GLENFIDDICH 12 YEAR (SCOTLAND) (G)
Another subsidiary of William Grant & Sons, Ltd, founded by
William Grant in 1887. Boasts continual use of original Robbie
Dhu spring. Aged in American oak and European ex- sherry cask.
Nose: Light, fragrant, pear, pine

Palate: Light body, medium sweet, citrusy, malt, grassy, chocolate, and peat smoke whisper
Finish: Soft, fruity nougat, vanilla
glenfiddich.com

DALLOWAY CHOCOLATE (USA) DOMINICAN REPUBLIC 72%
Profile: E &Fr
Muscular, but in a good way.
dallowaychocolate.com

BONNAT (FRANCE) PUERTO CABELLO, VZ 75%
Profile: Fr &S
Turns the chocolate to whiskey.
bonnat-chocolatier.com

DANDELION CHOCOLATE (USA) COSTA ESMERALDAS, ECUADOR 70%
Profile: Fr &E
Great mouthfeel together.
dandelionchocolate.com

AMEDEI (ITALY) CHUAO, VZ, 70% PROFILE: FR&E
Very worth trying as long as Amedei remains Amedei.
amedei.it

THE MACALLAN 12 YEAR, SHERRY OAK (SCOTLAND) (A)
The Macallan, located in Speyside, was among the first Scottish distilleries to be licensed. Alexander Reid, a barley farmer and school teacher founded Macallan in 1824. By 1892, Macallan began to be recognized outside of Scotland. It is famous for establishing a world record at auction in 2010, when The Macallan 64 Year in Lalique sold for $460,000, at Sotheby's in New York. The auction was for charity. The Macallan attributes the quality of its whiskies

to three things besides its master-distillers: "curiously small stills, which contribute to it's rich and fruity new spirit; taking only 16% of the final distillation (the best of the best cut) to fill their oak casks; and the casks themselves." They claim to "spend more on sourcing, building and caring for their casks than any other single malt whisky producer." On their website, they state the important source of their primary aromas and flavors lies in the wood, with the following 3 cask types giving rise to the respective flavor notes: Spanish oak sherry cask: chocolate, orange, dried fruits and spices; American oak sherry cask: sweet citrus, light spice, vanilla, light oak; and American oak bourbon barrels: sweet citrus, coconut, oaky. You can read more at themacallan.com

Nose: Vanilla, hint of ginger, dried fruits, sherry, wood smoke
Palate: Smooth, dried fruits, sherry, wood smoke and spice
Finish: Toffee, dried fruits, wood smoke and spice

BONNAT (FRANCE) LOS COLORADOS, ECUADOR 75%
Profile: N&Fr
So, so, so pleasing!
bonnat-chocolatier.com

PRALUS (FRANCE) MADAGASCAR 75% Profile: E&T
Brings out the roasty notes.
chocolats-pralus.com

MADECASSE (MADAGASCAR) 70%: Profile: T
Pops the fruit.
madecasse.com

MONKEY SHOULDER BLENDED MALT SCOTCH WHISKY (SCOTLAND) (E)
Technically not a single malt but a blend of three single malts, aged in first-fill ex-bourbon casks. Unlike other blends, Monkey

Shoulder contains no other grains. Monkey Shoulder is owned by
William Grant & Sons, Ltd. Visit their site at monkeyshoulder.com
Nose: Orange zest, vanilla, honey, spice, oak
Palate: Vanilla, spice
Finish: Smooth

DANDELION CHOCOLATE (USA) ZORZAL, DOMINICAN REPUBLIC 70%
Profile: E &Fr,
tobacco, walnut
Together, goes velvety mahogany
dandelionchocolate.com

FRESCO ARTISAN CHOCOLATE (USA) DOMINICAN REPUBLIC #224 72%
Profile: E&Fr
Boosts the whisky
frescochocolate.com

THEO MILK CHOCOLATE (USA) 45% (DARK MILK BLEND)
Profile: E & caramel
This milk has a whisper of fruit and spice. Add Monkey Shoulder
and you get a perfume that brings out fruit and brandy notes.
theochocolate.com

DEERHAMMER DISTILLERY
Founded by Amy and Lenny Eckstein in 2010, Deerhammer is
perhaps the highest altitude distillery anywhere, located at
8000 feet above sea level in Buena Vista, Colorado. Besides the
dry mountain air (30% humidity in the warehouse) and extreme
temperature fluctuations, Deerhammer's terroir includes the
whitewater currents of the Arkansas River. Lenny himself built the
distillery from used dairy equipment and repurposed machinery.
They also commissioned a Scottish-style direct-fire 140-gallon
copper pot still from Arkansas, made by someone who is called

"The Colonel." Deerhammer Single Malt Whiskey is their signature spirit, fermented in the open-air and matured in charred virgin white oak. Boasts a complex profile, with notes of coffee and chocolate, it's a distinctly American expression. Read more about Deerhammer at deerhammer.com

BEST MATES WITH DEERHAMMER AMERICAN SINGLE MALT WHISKEY (USA) (N-B)
Unique, high-altitude flavor profile created by using several types of malted barley and yeast strains.
Nose: Vanilla, butterscotch, caramel, honey, malt and herbal.
Palate: Orangey, spice, cocoa, coffee, vanilla, butter, menthol.
Finish: Long, with caramel, toffee and raisin

FRUITION CHOCOLATE (USA) HISPANIOLA, DOMINICAN REPUBLIC 68%
Profile: E&Fr&S
Turns up peanut.
tastefruition.com

CASTRONOVO CHOCOLATE (USA), SIERRA NEVADA, COLUMBIA 72%
Profile: FF Excellent.
castronovochocolate.com

LETTERPRESS (USA), UCAYALI , PERU 70%
Profile: S&H&Fr
Adds pepper to the spice palate. Wonderful!
letterpresschocolate.com

RANGER CHOCOLATE (USA), SAN MARTIN , PERU 70%
Profile: S&H
rangerchocolate.com

WESTLAND DISTILLERY
Co-founded in 2010 by Matthew Hoffman and Emerson Lamb. Lamb exited, but Hoffman remains as Westland's exciting, innovative master distiller. He realized that the coastal area of Washington State had many climate and ecological similarities to Scotland, where he studied distilling while earning a masters degree. Hoffman started by using imported Scottish peat in their signature single malt, but is committed to using regional ingredients, including malted barley and Oregon oak. Westland expects to release a single malt made with local peat in 2020. Westland was named Distillery of the Year in 2015 by the American Distillery Institute. Rémy Cointreau (owners of Bruichladdich) acquired the distillery in 2017. In considering the sale, Hoffman was encouraged by the high quality that Bruichladdich has been able to maintain as a subsidiary of Rémy Cointreau. Learn more about Westland at westlanddistillery.com

BEST MATES WITH WESTLAND AMERICAN SINGLE MALT WHISKEY (USA) (N-B)
Nose: Includes citrus, floral whisper, chocolate custard cream, honey and malt
Palate: Creamy with orange, cherry, chocolate, and almond
Finish: Coffee

LETTERPRESS, BELIZE, 70% Profile: E&Fr&S
Quirky, goes peppery.
letterpresschocolate.com

LETTERPRESS, UCAYALI 70% Profile :S&H&Fr
Changes the whiskey body to medium heavy. Interesting effect.
letterpresschocolate.com

BONNAT (FRANCE), XOCONUSCO, MEXICO 75%
Profile: N
Goes dark and cereal.
bonnat-chocolatier.com

BEST MATES WITH WESTLAND AMERICAN SINGLE MALT WHISKEY, SHERRY WOOD (N- B/S)
A New World take on the Scottish tradition, Westland finishes in
Pedro Ximénez and Oloroso sherry casks.
Nose: Honey, baked goods, raisin, maple syrup, banana
Palate: Maple and raisin syrupy notes
Finish: Yellow fruits.

MICHEL CLUIZEL (FRANCE) VILA GRACINDA 67%
Profile: E & honey
Whiskey adds muscularity, wood, Butterfinger® bar center.
cluizel.com

TWENTY-FOUR BLACKBIRDS ARTISAN CHOCOLATE (USA), OKO CARIBE, DOMINICAN REPUBLIC 75% Profile:E
Goes sarsaparilla and mellow wood.
twentyfourblackbirds.com

DANDELION CHOCOLATE (USA), KOKOA KAMILLI, TANZANIA, 70%
Profile: FF&T&E
Excellent. The chocolate brings out oak and malt.
dandelionchocolate.com

THEO CHOCOLATE (USA) MILK CHOCOLATE 45%
Profile: E with caramel
The chocolate brings out the malty side of the whiskey and the
whiskey adds depth to the caramel notes.
theochocolate.com

12

SPIRITED PAIRINGS:
CHOCOLATE AND NORTH AMERICAN BOURBONS & RYE WHISKEYS

If I cannot drink bourbon and smoke cigars in Heaven, then I shall not go."
—Mark Twain

CHOCOLATE & CLASSIC BOURBON (N1) (*=MINNICK SUBCATEGORY)

BUFFALO TRACE DISTILLERY

The name, Buffalo Trace, refers to the path the buffalo took westward. Owned by the Sazerac Company since 1992, Buffalo Trace is home to premier American whiskey lines, including: Eagle Rare, Blantons, Van Winkle, E. H. Taylor, Jr., Stagg, Jr., Benchmark, W. L. Weller, Sazerac Rye, and several others. The distillery is on the National Registry of Historic Landmarks and traces its origins to the second decade of the 19th Century - a 200–year legacy.

The distillery complex is a popular stop along the National Landmark Tour. Learn more about their brands and fascinating history at **buffalotracedistillery.com**

BEST MATES WITH BUFFALO TRACE KENTUCKY STRAIGHT WHISKEY (N1) (*N)
Tasting notes are from the Buffalo Trace website:
Nose: Vanilla, mint and molasses.
Palate: Brown sugar, spice, oak, toffee, dark fruit and anise.
Finish: Long and smooth with depth.

FRUITION CHOCOLATE (USA) HISPANIOLA, DOMINICAN REPUBLIC 68%
Profile: E&Fr&S
Yes! We know this one goes well with bourbon.
tastefruition.com

PUMP STREET BAKERY (UK), GRENADA , 70% Profile: FF
Brings out the honey. If you can get Buffalo Trace across the pond, do!
pumpstreetbakery.com

DALLOWAY CHOCOLATE (USA), DOMINICAN REPUBLIC Profile: E&Fr
Goes muscular, but in a good way.
dallowaychocolate.com

CASTRONOVO (USA), AMAZONAS, VZ , 72% Profile: N
An interesting bar on its own, it really opens up with the Buffalo.
castronovochocolate.com

BEST MATES WITH LARCENY VERY SPECIAL SMALL BATCH 7 YEAR (N-1) (*C)

WOODBLOCK CHOCOLATE (USA), BALAO , ECUADOR 70% PROFILE: S&H
If you like hot cinnamon.
woodblockchocolate.com

PRALUS (FRANCE), VENEZUELA (BARLOVENTO) 75% PROFILE: FR& ROASTY (E)
More than acceptable combo.
chocolats-pralus.com

KINGS COUNTY DISTILLERY
Kings is a visitor-friendly distillery located in the Brooklyn Navy Yard, steps away from the Brooklyn Whiskey Wars of the 1860s. Founded in 2010, they were the first distillery to open its doors in New York City since Prohibition. To visit them, book a tour at kingscountydistillery.com

BEST MATES WITH KINGS COUNTY BOURBON (N-1) (*G)
This is a 2 year (minimally aged) straight bourbon, young and grain forward. At 90 proof, it is surprisingly mild.
Nose: Classic caramel and vanilla nose with orange whisper.
Palate: Corn-fed sweet palate, a light overlay of licorice. To me, more Demerara than molasses, mild baking spices with smidgen of heat.

MAROU FAISEURS DE CHOCOLAT(VIETNAM), TIEN GIANG 80%
PROFILE: S&H
Makes for a muscle drink!
marouchocolate.com

CREO CHOCOLATE (USA), HEIRLOOM HACIENDA LIMON, ECUADOR 73%
PROFILE: Fr & E & nut & honey-caramel
Adds depth to both partners
creochocolate.com

FRUITION CHOCOLATE (USA) HISPANIOLA, DOMINICAN REPUBLIC 68%
PROFILE: T
The sweetness counter-punches the high alcohol content and
goes caramel-maple
tastefruition.com

BONNAT (FRANCE) ASFRATH (DARK) MILK 65% PROFILE: S & H
Really pops licorice!
bonnat-chocolatier.com

TUTHILLTOWN SPIRITS FARM DISTILLERY

Ralph Erenzo and Brian Lee founded Tuthilltown Spirits LLC in
2003 and converted a 220 –year- old mill granary into a micro-
distillery in the beautiful Hudson Valley. They began by making
vodka from local apples and they still use ingredients farmed
within ten miles. Their products include gin, vodka, whiskey,
liquors and bitters. William Grant & Sons, the Scottish Distilling
company, now own Tuthilltown. Visitors are welcome at the
distillery, restaurant and shop. Find out more at tuthilltown.com.

BEST MATES WITH TUTHILLTOWN, HUDSON BABY BOURBON (N1)(*G)

Nose: sweet corn with a hint of vanilla.
Palate: light and sweet with a whisper of ginger.
Finish: light

BAR AU CHOCOLAT (USA) DUARTE PROVINCE, DOMINICAN REPUBLIC 70%
Profile: FF
Punches up the bourbon, in a very good way.
barauchocolat.com

FRUITION CHOCOLATE (USA) HISPANIOLA, DOMINICAN REPUBLIC 68%
Profile: T & Cherry vanilla and a top whisper of mint.
tastefruition.com

BEST MATES WITH KNOB CREEK SMALL BATCH 9 YEAR KENTUCKY STRAIGHT BOURBON (N1) (*CI)

QUON (JAPAN), SAO TOME 66%
Profile: Earthy roast
Smooths out the bourbon.
quon-choco.com

MADECASSE (MADAGASCAR) 70% PROFILE: T
Goes maple.
madecassse.com

LINDT EXCELLENCE (SWITZERLAND) 70% PROFILE: E & CARAMEL & Fr
Goes cognac. Nice! lindtusa.com

GREEN & BLACKS (UK) DARK 70%
Profile: Earthy roast& Fr & S
Cools out the spiciness of the whiskey, and the whiskey pops the spice in the chocolate.
greenandblacks.com

BEST MATES WITH BLACK DIRT, NEW YORK STRAIGHT BOURBON (N1)
Black Dirt Distillery is located in Pine Island, New York. Their products preceded the opening of their micro-distillery in 2013.

They produce bourbon in small batches from numbered, single barrels. The distillery takes its name from the dark soil that covers thousands of acres in upstate New York. An ancient glacial lake bequeathed a soil perfect for growing the corn that they use in their bourbon. The mash bill is 80% corn, 12% malted barley, and 8% rye. Visit their website at **blackdistillery.com**

Nose: Cereal, oak, vanilla

Palate: Light body, dry, toasty grain, fruity, chocolate, espresso, spicy

Finish: Long, hint of smoke, rye spice

DANDELION CHOCOLATE (USA), ZORZAL, DOMINICAN REPUBLIC 70%

Profile: E & FR

Tobacco, berry, trails raw walnut. Adds notes of maple-caramel

dandelionchocolate.com

DICK TAYLOR CRAFT CHOCOLATE (USA) BELIZE 70% Profile: FF

Interesting effect. Turns the plum and sweet cherry to dried fruit, adds Bordeaux wine grapes and wood.

dicktaylorchocolate.com

A JAPANESE BOURBON?

Technically no! Only made-in America bourbon whiskeys can legally call themselves bourbon. This is bourbon-style. Japan acquired whisky making from the Scots in the early 20th century. For the main part, that means single malts and more traditional blends. However, they also make spirit from rice. Instead of using single yeasts during fermentation, the Japanese use various ones creatively. Their water tends to create a spirit that is smooth on the palate. These are whiskies that demonstrate balance, delicacy and a high degree of food compatibility. Today, Japan is making some of the world's best whiskies that, justifiably, command hefty prices.

Suntory, Nikka, Hibiki—if you can try them, do! You can match their sherried single malts and blends to chocolates similarly to the way you would to their Scottish counterparts, think Macallan, Balvnie, Glenlivet. For a more typical, affordable Japanese whisky, in the Scottish style, try Shinshu Mars Iwai Tradition. However, the Shinshu Mars whisky matched here is the Iwai Whisky (not the Tradition). Nevertheless, it will give you a sense of Japanese terroir.

BEST MATES WITH SHINSHU MARS IWAI JAPANESE WHISKY (JAPAN) (N1)

Located in the Japanese alps region near Nagano at an altitude of 2,600 feet (798 meters), the pure local water and oak contribute to the terroir of this whisky. Corn dominant (75% corn, 25% barley) it is aged in ex-bourbon barrels.
Nose: Vanilla, oak, light fruit
Palate: Creamy, vanilla, lychee, quince, pear, suggestion of red fruit.
Finish: Short and subtle

FRUITION CHOCOLATE (USA) MARAÑON, PERU 76%

Profile: T & nut
The Iwai takes this 76% sweeter, suppressing the walnut notes while bringing out red fruit and grapefruit notes in this 2016 harvest.
tastefuition.com

BONNAT (FRANCE) PUERTO CABELLO , VZ 75%

Profile: FR&S
Turns mellow, aged wood.
bonnat-chocolatier.com

PRALUS , BARLOVENTO , VZ 75%
Profile: Fr & Earthy roast.
A cut above. chocolat-pralus.com

PUMP STREET BAKERY (UK) GRENADA, 70% PROFILE: FF
pumpstreetbakery.com

FRUITION CHOCOLATE (USA) WILD BOLIVIA 74%
Profile: Earthy roast & honey
Whispers of grain in both almost cancel each other out and leave behind an overall pleasing effect.
tastefruition.com

CHOCOLATE & WHEATED BOURBONS (N2)

BEST MATES WITH W. L. WELLER SPECIAL RESERVE (N2) (*C)
W. L. Weller created the wheated bourbon niche, replacing rye in the mash bill. Now Weller whiskeys belong to the Buffalo Trace line. Weller whiskeys are said to be made just like the Van Winkles, but they're aged in a different (less optimal, allegedly) part of the warehouse. Their 12 Year is supposed to be superior to the Special Reserve and closer to the Van Winkles–but try to find one! They are released only a couple times a year and rationed out. Let this one breathe 15 minutes and lovely aromas begin to show up.

These are my own notes for the Special Reserve :
Nose: apple, hint of leather, caramel, butterscotch
Palate: caramel, vanilla, turns to cinnamon and pepper, some oaky-herbal undernotes
Finish: peppery, oaky-herbal undernotes, caramelized walnut trail

BAR AU CHOCOLAT (USA), DUARTE PROVINCE, DOMINICAN REPUBLIC 70%
Profile: FF
Superb combination. Several Bar Au Chocolat origins really work well with this high wheat bourbon.
barauchocolat.com

BAR AU CHOCOLAT (USA), MADAGASCAR 70 %
Profile: T &Fr
Pops raspberry.
barauchocolat.com

BAR AU CHOCOLATE (USA), COSTA RICA 72%
Profile: Earthy roast (coffee) & grain & berry
Also excellent.
barauchocolat.com

FRENCH BROAD CHOCOLATES (USA), GUATEMALA 73%
Profile: E&Fr
Brings out oat.
frenchbroadchocolates.com

BONNAT (FRANCE) LOS COLORADOS, ECUADOR 75%
Profile: N & hint of fruit.
bonnat-chocolatier.com

BEST MATES WITH BERNHEIM ORIGINAL 7 YEAR SMALL BATCH WHISKEY (N2)
Bernheim is a wheat whiskey and not a bourbon.

CHARM SCHOOL CHOCOLATE (USA) BELIZE, 70%
Profile: E&Fr& hint of twang
Turns to berry liquor
charmschoolchocolate.com

DOMORI (ITALY), APURIMAC, PERU 70%
Profile: E
domori.com

BEST MATES WITH EAGLE RARE 10 YEAR (N2 R&O) (*N)
A rich and oaky expression from Buffalo Trace. One of the great American bourbons at an amazing value. Here are the official tasting notes from the Buffalo Trace website:
www.buffalotrace.com
Nose: Aromas of toffee, hints of orange peel, herbs, honey, leather and oak.
Palate: Bold and dry, delicate notes of candied almonds and rich cocoa.
Finish: Dry and lingering.

DALLOWAY CHOCOLATE (USA) DOMINICAN REPUBLIC 72%
Profile: E &Fr
Luxuriously rich!
dallowaychocolate.com

BAR AU CHOCOLATE (USA) DUARTE PROVINCE, DOMINICAN REPUBLIC 70%
Profile: FF
Also very good.
barauchocolat.com

RITUAL CHOCOLATE (USA), BALAO, ECUADOR 75%
Profile: EARTHY ROAST &S&H
ritualchocolate.com

FRENCH BROAD CHOCOLATES (USA) CACAO BISIESTO, NICARAGUA 68%
Profile: S&H
Sugar and herb, tea and coffee.
frenchbroadchocolates.com

CASTRONOVO CHOCOLATE (USA) HONDURAS, THE LOST CITY, 72%
Profile: E & nut
Brings out licorice notes.
castronovochocolate.com

CREO CHOCOLATE (USA) HACIENDA LÍMON, ECUADOR, 73%
Profile: E & Fr
creochocolate.com

PALETTE DE BINE (CANADA) POLOCHIC VALLEY, GUATEMALA, 70%
Profile: Fr
Goes so rich, so fudgy... and maple (but no maple in this bar!).
palettedebine.com

BEST MATES WITH BREUCKELEN 77 WHEAT WHISKEY (N2)
Breuckelen is the old Dutch spelling for Brooklyn where this craft
distillery began in 2010. Besides whiskeys, they also produce gin.
The 77 Wheat Whiskey is 100% wheat, aged 1–2 years. They are
committed to using local ingredients.
Nose: Herbal, malt, oak, char, caramel, toffee, citrus zest
Palate: Thin, caramel, sweet grain, Demerara sugar, vanilla, wood,
spicy center, smooth at the edges
Finish: Caramel, oak
brkdistilling.com

FRUITION CHOCOLATE (USA) HISPANIOLA, DOMINICAN REPUBLIC, 68%
Profile: E&Fr&S
tastefruition.com

SOL CACAO (USA), ECUADOR, CEDEÑO FARM 70%
Profile: E&T
Turns up the whiskey in a flavorful way.
solcacao.com

FRUITION CHOCOLATE (USA), MARAÑON, PERU 76%
Profile: T & nut
tastefruition.com

FRUITION CHOCOLATE (USA), HEIRLOOM COSTA RICA 74%
Profile: T
Brings up brandy notes.
tastefruition.com

FRESCO ARTISAN CHOCOLATE (USA), DOMINICAN REPUBLIC #224
Profile: E & Fr
Goes hearty.
frescochocolate.com

WYOMING WHISKEY
Located in Kirby, Wyoming, this distillery uses regional ingredients, from its limestone water to its local Non-GMO grain. Enjoy the beautiful video on their website: wyomingwhiskey.com

BEST MATES WITH WYOMING WHISKEY SMALL BATCH BOURBON (N2)
Tasting Notes from the company:
Nose: Floral, vanilla and caramel
Palate: Floral with baking spices, browned butter, vanilla, caramel, and cinnamon, mouthfeel is light and smooth with vanilla bean and cinnamon spice filling the mouth cavity, hint of mint.
Finish: Medium length finish with toffee. Spice and vanilla fade.

FRENCH BROAD CHOCOLATES (USA) COSTA RICA 80%
Profile: E & Fr trails nuts
frenchbroadchocolates.com

MADÉCAASSE (MADAGASCAR) 80%
Profile: T
madécasse.com

RITUAL CHOCOLATE (USA), BALAO, ECUADOR 75%
Profile: Roast E & S&H
Takes a very pleasant turn.
ritualchocolate.com

CHOCOLATE & HIGH RYE BOURBONS (N1/3)

BEST MATES WITH WOODFORD RESERVE DISTILLERS SELECT KENTUCKY STRAIGHT BOURBON (USA) (N1/3) (*C)
Woodford Reserve is a subsidiary of Brown-Forman. Their master distiller since 2003 is Chris Morris, who is responsible for much of the innovation at Woodford. He created the world's first bourbon finished in Chardonnay and Pinot Noir barrels. He also experimented with maple barrels. This bourbon is 90.4 proof with 72% corn, 18% rye and 10% barley.
Tasting notes according to the website:
Nose: Dried fruit, hints of mint and oranges covered with a dusting of cocoa. Faint vanilla and tobacco spice.
Taste: Rich, citrus, cinnamon and cocoa. Toffee, caramel, chocolate and spice notes.
Finish: Smooth, almost creamy and long.
woodfordreserve.com

CREO CHOCOLATE (USA) HACIENDA LÍMON, ECUADOR 73%

Profile: E & Fr, honey-caramel

Beautifully textured chocolate works well for this bourbon.

creochocolate.com

SOMA (CANADA) CSB CHAMA, VZ. 70%

Profile: N & Fr

Brings out cherry.

somachocolate.com

CHOCOLATE & RYE WHISKEY (N3)

BEST MATES WITH CROWN ROYAL NORTHERN HARVEST BLENDED CANADIAN RYE (CANADA) (N3)

Crown Royal is produced solely at the Crown Royal distillery at Gimli, on the shores of Lake Winnipeg, Manitoba, Canada. Crown Royal is a subsidiary of Diageo.

Nose: Floral, apple, honey , grainy.

Palate: Apple, cherry, citrus, vanilla, spice, pepper

Finish: Long, fruity, woody, spicy

HUMMINGBIRD CHOCOLATE MAKER(CANADA), CAP-HAÏTIEN 70%

Profile: Fr &E

Tea and lychee notes.

hummingbirdchocolate.com

HUMMINGBIRD CHOCOLATE MAKER (CANADA), COPAN, HONDURAS 70%

Profile: E

Coffee, nut, caramelized demearara Floral notes bloom.

hummingbirdchocolate.com

BEST MATES WITH BREUCKELEN 77 RYE & CORN (USA) (N3)
This is a rye composed of 90% rye and 10% corn.
Nose: Floral, herbal, juniper (they do make gin!)
Palate: Hint of the medicinal, rye spice, sweet, caramel
Finish: Dry, spicy

FRUITION CHOCOLATE (USA) WILD BOLIVIA 74%, LIMITED RELEASE
Profile: E (roast) & honey
Whiskey brings out fruit.
tastefruition.com

FRESCO ARTISAN CHOCOLATE (USA) DOMINICAN REPUBLIC #224 72%
Profile: E & Fr
Brings out the caramel.
frescochocolate.com

FRUITION CHOCOLATE (USA) HISPANIOLA 68%
Profile: E & FR & S
Caramel turns to maple sugar, quite sweet
tastefruition.com

CALDERA DISTILLERY (CANADA)
Caldera Distillery is located in River John, Nova Scotia, historically a shipbuilding community. Caldera grows their own grain on the distillery land. They are committed to transparency, but there's little information on their website. Hmm. They distill whisky and rum.
caldera.ca

BEST MATES WITH CALDERA HURRICANE 5 (CANADA) (N3)
Hurricane 5 is a blended rye whisky. The name reflects a storm that struck in October 1939 that was historically recorded as Hurricane #5.

Nose: Fruity rye spice, ginger
Palate: Smooth, sweet, caramel, oak, citrus
Finish: Medium length, clove, ginger, pepper

HUMMINGBIRD CHOCOLATE MAKER (CA), COPAN, HONDURAS 70%

Profile: E & Roast
(coffee, nuts, caramel)
Hurricane 5 brings out subtler, caramelized Demerara.
hummingbirdchocolate.com

PALETTE DE BINE (CANADA), HAÏTI-PISA 70% Profile: Fr & nut

palettedebine.com

MAROU FAISEURS DE CHOCOLAT (VIETNAM) TIEN GIANG 70%

Profile: S&H
Pops fruit, despite a little burn.
marouchocolate.com

HUMMINGBIRD CHOCOLATE MAKER (CANADA) OKO CARIBE, HISPANIOLA, D. R. 70%

Profile: Fr
hummingbirdchocolate.com

BAR AU CHOCOLAT (USA) DUARTE PROVINCE, DOMINICAN REPUBLIC 70%

Profile: FF
Goes cinnamon and vanilla.
barauchocolat.com

BEST MATES WITH TUTHILLTOWN HUDSON MANHATTAN RYE (USA) (N3)

The first rye to be produced in New York State since prohibition, it's pleasing and appropriate for pairing. This spirit is 92 proof and 100% rye. Made for cocktails, it dresses up nicely as a hot

date for chocolate.
Nose: Maple and light mint.
Palate: Mint, clove and pepper spice.
Finish: Clove and cinnamon

.

CREO CHOCOLATE (USA) HEIRLOOM HACIENDA LÍMON, ECUADOR 70%
Profile: E & Fr
(red fruit, nuts, honey, caramel)
creochocolate.com

RITUAL CHOCOLATE (USA), BALAO, ECUADOR 75%
Profile: E & S&H
ritualchocolate.com

BEST MATES WITH CARIBOU CROSSING (CANADA/USA) (N3)
The Caribou Crossing website states its whisky is "the world's first single barrel Canadian whisky." Caribou Crossing, 80 proof, was selected by Sazerac's master–blender, Drew Mayville, and is bottled in Kentucky by Sazerac/Buffalo Trace. It is a blended whisky, married from the spirits of several Canadian distilleries. Each barrel may vary. However, the rye component (N3) is the Profile to match. This is a thoroughly pleasing whisky that demonstrates the subtlety of Canadian rye.

My tasting notes:
Nose: Floral rye, spice, maple, cherry brandy, butterscotch, vanilla, and just a hint of varnish
Flavor: Creamy, fruity, smooth, peppermint, rye spice, oak, vanilla
Finish: Medium length, exits on oak, cherry, mild spice

HUMMINGBIRD (CANADA) COPAN, HONDURAS 70 %
Profile: E &roast coffee & nut & caramelized Demerara
Gives rise to fudge and caramel.
hummingbirdchocolate.com

HUMMINGBIRD (CANADA) CAP-HATIEN 70% Profile: Fr & E & tea
Goes dark, deep cherry cough drop.
hummingbirdchocolate.com

SOMA CHOCOLATEMAKER (CANADA) CSB CHAMA, VZ 70 %
Profile: N& Fr
Brings out rich nuttiness.
somachocolate.com

LOT NO. 40, 100% POT STILL CANADIAN RYE WHISKY (CANADA)
2017 edition, not the celebrated 2012 release, which took the whisky
world by storm. For more history, read Davin de Kergommeaux at
canadianwhisky.org.

Still an excellent whisky. Produced by Corby at Hiram Walker
(Pernod-Ricard) in Ontario. Named 2015 Canadian Whisky of the
Year and won 2016 San Francisco World Spirits Competition, Double
Gold for Best Canadian Whisky. No age statement, basically a 7-8
year old. This is a 100% rye, and that grain is certainly apparent.
But, to my nose, was not the dramatic, bakery fresh bread noted
by reviewers of earlier releases, although after long breathing,
some loaves did appear. First pouring produced cloud of rapturous
floral and hot trending spice notes rather than baking spices.

Nose: moving from top down, floral, licorice, chocolate, orange
rind, caraway- rye seed, and the bread loaves in the middle.
Palate: caramel forward all the way, sweet, coats tongue and hangs

in, hot cinnamon spice now subdued, whisper of almond, vanilla takes a back seat.
Finish: quite long, with fading caraway-rye notes, sweet caramel and orange rind lingering.

BEST MATE WITH LOT #40 (N3) (*C)
Try this with chocolate that has a strong earthy component.

DANDELION CHOCOLATE (USA), ZORZAL, DOMINICAN REPUBLIC 70%
Profile: E & FR
(tobacco, berry, trails raw walnut)
Brings out the rye breadbasket! Weighty and wonderful, not for people timid about flavor.
dandelionchocolate.com

WYOMING WHISKEY OUTRYDER (USA) (N3)
Made from two separate mash bills distilled in 2011, Outryder is not a bourbon. It's considered high rye, but not high enough to be a true rye.

The company's tasting notes:
Nose: brown baking spices of cinnamon and allspice with creamy browned butter
Palate: clove and allspice, freshly baked dark rye bread with hints of orange blossom honey
Mouthfeel: cinnamon spice with creamy butterscotch pudding
Finish: long, spicy rye finish coupled with hints of buttery toffee

BEST MATES WITH WYOMING WHISKEY OUTRYDER (N3)

WOODBLOCK CHOCOLATE (USA) BALAO, ECUADOR 70%
Profile: S&H
Turns delightfully maple and cocoa.
woodblockchocolte.com

BONNAT (FRANCE) PUERTO CABELLO , VZ
Profile: Fr & S
bonnat-chocolatier.com

13

MUST TRY-BEFORE-YOU-DIE CHOCOLATE MAKERS

More than any other food, chocolate delights and enchants ... chocolate tantalizes and it comforts. Chocolate has soothed fretful children and welcomed tired travelers; mountain climbers have saved their last piece of chocolate to celebrate reaching new heights; suitors have given chocolate to show the depth of their devotion. Chocolate has been used as a stimulant, an aphrodisiac, and even a form of currency.
—Neva Beach

IF YOU'RE LOOKING FOR A LIST of the top 20 best chocolate makers, you're not going to find it here. Oh, I have indeed listed 20 here. And I can truly say they are fabulous. But I'm not going to say that these 20 are the best in the world, or even in North America. To me that seems an arrogant over-reach. Who am I—the omniscient chocolate queen who knights chocolate makers on the pages of my book?

Some are consistently good, others have only managed to nail an occasional bar that merits accolades. Many bars that I've loved, but have not included in this book, include those made by: Rogue (USA), Amano (USA), Guittard (USA) Zotter (Austria) and Rózarölgyi (Hungary). I love these chocolate makers! If you can get your hands on their bars, please try them on their own or follow the guidance of the flavor profiles to pair with whiskeys. I've also liked a few Japanese chocolate makers with distinctive styles (a subject for a future blog). But there many others. So many! Mostly, their lack of representation in this book was simply due to not being able to get my hands on their bars when I was running my pairing tests. Timing is everything!

Most of the neglected chocolate makers will eventually find their way into my evolving database. Hopefully, I'll get to blog about them at some point. There are also barsmiths known only regionally. I regret that there are international chocolate makers I've heard great things about but have never been able to find in New York. Imagine something you cannot find in New York! It's rare, but it happens. And it's humbling. Maybe we New Yorkers only think our city is the center of the universe. When I can't get my hands on a particular brand, I feel disappointed, if not down-right deprived. But as more bars are exported, as I manage to make my way to a chocolate festival here or there, or some generous soul gifts me a bar after their travels, more bars will make it into my database, and perhaps even into my blog, R. M. Peluso Riffs on Chocolate, which can be accessed on my website ctm-chocolate-tasting-meditation.com

You've already been introduced to a number of important whiskey makers. Now, let me tell you about some of those great chocolate makers whose bars have already been paired with the whiskeys in this book. The 20 listed below have been selected from those companies still directed by owner-operators whose personal guidance provides integrity and quality to their brand. "The proof of the pudding is in the eating," so goes the saying. Make that "The proof of the chocolate is in the tasting." The list here has been drawn from those whose chocolates worked best and most frequently with the whiskeys in this book. But the bars of these chocolate makers first had to please my taste buds, unaccompanied by any other food or beverage, in the morning, on my "virgin palate." All but one of these barsmiths have produced award-winning chocolate. The one that hasn't—yet!—has won an award in my heart anyway. Most have exemplary policies of corporate responsibility and stand for purity of ingredients, conservation of the rainforests, and economic justice for cacao farmers and their communities. Most source their beans carefully, often directly from farmers or cooperatives. These chocolate makers have been my community, some for over a decade now. I love these people. And you will love their bars.

INTERNATIONAL CHOCOLATE MAKERS

SOMA CHOCOLATEMAKER (CANADA)

David Castellan and Cynthia Leung founded Soma in 2003. They were among the first wave of the North American craft chocolate movement. Soma welcomes visitors at two shops in Toronto. Fortunately, for those of us who do not live nearby, they also have a robust online business. There are rare retailers who carry their bars. Try The Meadow, in New York City and Chocolopolis, Seattle. Soma creates micro-batches of elegant, single origin and blended bars (see if you can spot the maple leaf on the front of the bars), but also drinking chocolate, truffles, cookies, and gelato during the summer (no, that you cannot order online!). Enjoy the creative product descriptions on their website at somachocolate.com

BONNAT- CHOCOLATIER (FRANCE)

The award-winning Chocolate Bonnat tradition began several generations ago, in 1884, by dessert-maker Felix Bonnat, in Voiron, France. Felix had the foresight to acquire an early chocolate conching machine. La Maison Bonnat today is led by Stéphane Bonnat whose father, Raymond, was the first in the family to make chocolate bars as end products for consumers. Stéphane went on to firmly establish the single origin grand crus. You can find more information about the family history on the website, if you read French. The texture of Bonnat bars is incomparably luxurious. Easily found in France, Bonnat is carried by a number of gourmet shops in New York, perhaps in a city near you, too. Visit: bonnat- chocolatier.com

CHOCOLAT PRALUS (FRANCE)

Before I ever thought of training to be a reviewer, I attended a chocolate show, and tasted Pralus's famous pyramid of single origin chocolates. Pralus hit me like a bolt of lightning, and I can still remember the distinct regional flavors and my reactions to them. These bars were formative in my early understanding of terroir. Pralus tends to produce 75% dark, with aromas and flavors that are clear and assertive about their identities. When I finally met Francois Pralus years later, I was able to express my gratitude to him for his contribution to my life in chocolate. Francois is the son of an award winning pastry chef, Auguste Pralus. Like Robert Steinberg of Scharffen Berger, Francois trained at Bernachon, and decided he would make his own bean-to-bar chocolates. Pralus operates several shops in France, with the main factory in Roanne, taking over his father's original boutique. Francois sources chocolate from all over the world and now owns his own cacao estate in Madagascar. Read more here at chocolats-pralus.com

MAROU CHOCOLATE, FAISEURS DE CHOCOLAT (VIETNAM)

What happens when two young Frenchmen meet in Vietnam? They start a chocolate company, of course! Vincent Mourou-Rochebois and Samuel Maruta founded Marou in 2011, sourcing their cacao exclusively in Vietnam and operating their factory in Ho Chi Minh City (formerly Saigon). Cacao was first brought to Vietnam in the 19th century–who knew? It's mostly been a failed history, however, Marou has been changing that legacy. Vincent explains that Vietnamese cacao has a sour basis rather than a bitter one to which most of us are accustomed. These bars have lovely spice notes along with fruit and floral aromas. Vietnamese chocolate is definitely different from what you're used to, even if you're familiar with great artisan chocolate. An experience not to be missed! Visit their website at marouchocolate.com

AKESSON'S (UK)

Pick up a chocolate bar made from Madagascar beans, and there's a good chance the beans originated on one of Akesson's estates. The son of a Swedish diplomat who later settled in Madagascar, Bertil Akesson is now based in London. He began as a planter, selling beans to leading chocolate makers throughout the USA and Europe, then began making his own bars in France in 2009. Overall, Bertil spends a lot of time traveling the globe to bring us delectable chocolate. His cacao is grown on a few estates in the Sambirano Valley in the Northwest part of Madagascar, an area known for its flavorful cacao since the 1920s, and in the Mata Atlantica wild forest area of Brazil. He also creates bars from beans grown by the Sukrama family in Bali. Social, ecological and economic sustainability are corporate values. Learn more at akessons-organic.com

PUMP STREET BAKERY (UK)

Pump Street Bakery is a family-owned bakery and cafe in Orford, England, on Suffolk's "Heritage Coast." They've been taking home awards for their single origin chocolates since 2015. To find a shop near you that sells their bars or to order online try pumpstreetbakery.com

PALETTE DE BINE (CANADA)

In Mont-Tremblant, Quebec, Canada, owner-operator Christine Blais began making chocolate in 2013 and opened her boutique-workshop in 2014. Her Palette de Bine bars won Gold and Silver awards in 2016 at the International Chocolate Awards and the Academy of Chocolate. Her unique, wood-bark, mold design and eco-friendly packaging honor the natural world of cacao. Visit: palettedebine.com

HUMMINGBIRD CHOCOLATE MAKER (CANADA)

Located in Almonte, Ontario, Hummingbird was founded in 2012 by owner- operators, Drew and Erica Gilmore. Their chocolate has been winning awards since 2014. Find a store that carries their bars in Canada and New York, or order online at: hummingbirdchocolate.com

UNITED STATES

FRUITION CHOCOLATE (USA)

Located in New York State's Catskill Mountain region, about a 2-hour drive from New York City, Fruition's owner-operator is Bryan Graham. Bryan was a pastry prodigy, promoted to pastry chef by the age of 18. After studying at the Culinary Institute of America, he trained with Jacques Torres and Chef Peter Greweling. Bryan founded Fruition in 2011, and is considered by many to be one of the top barsmiths in the United States. Fruition took home World Gold Best in Competition at the 2016 International

Chocolate Awards' Americas and Asia Pacific competition. The Grahams operate a workshop-store in Shokan and a satellite shop just up the road in Woodstock. Fruition raises money for his wife's (Dahlia Graham) charity: <u>corazondedahlia.org</u> from sales of its Corazon Milk Chocolate Quinoa Crunch bars to benefit Peruvian children and families. Fruition bars and unique confections can be found in select gourmet and chocolate specialty stores, but, for a sure thing, you can shop their online store at: <u>tastefruition.com</u>

ASKINOSIE CHOCOLATE (USA)

When it comes to corporate responsibility, giving back to his Springfield, Missouri community and to those from where he sources his cacao beans, perhaps no one tops Shawn Askinosie. Shawn was a successful criminal defense attorney before launching Askinosie Chocolate in 2005. His company has since been recognized by Forbes as "One of the 25 Best Small Companies in America." Askinoise works directly with farming communities on 4 continents, sharing profits and sustainably feeding over 1600 students in Tanzania and the Philippines. At home, his Chocolate University teaches local school children about chocolate-making and takes many of these students to the cacao farms abroad every summer. If this sounds like a man with a spiritual mission, you'd be correct. Shawn is Family Brother at Assumption Abbey, a Trappist monastic order. That's a lot of do-gooding, but it still comes down to making great chocolate. Get yours here at <u>askinosie.com</u>

FRENCH BROAD (USA)

When I first heard their name, I thought the owner was– well, a French woman! I later came to learn that the French Broad is a river that runs through Asheville, North Carolina, where Jael and Dan Rattigan run their workshop, store and cafe. French Broad's brick-and-mortar and online stores carry an impressive line of excellent craft chocolates. Their website is a great place to shop if you can't find the bars you want nearby. If you want to distinguish your products in the marketplace, you need a good story. French Broad tells their own charming history on their website. I won't be a spoiler. Go, read, visit: frenchbroadchocolates.com

DANDELION CHOCOLATE (USA)

When Todd Masonis and Cameron Ring sold their company, Plaxo, a social contact service, to Comcast in 2008, they soon decided to create a company where people could learn about how chocolate is made. They cofounded Dandelion in the Mission District of San Francisco. Though they started out as a "small batch" producer, the company has grown fast, with a factory and stores in Japan as well as their factory and cafe in San Francisco. They conduct tours and classes at their Valencia Street location. Their strong commitment to chocolate education can also be seen on a visit to their informational website. I love to check in often to learn new things at: dandelionchocolate.com

PATRIC CHOCOLATE (USA)

Founded in 2006 by its owner-operator, Alan "Patric" McClure had spent time in France before returning home to try to replicate quality chocolate of the kind he had sampled abroad. Bitten by the chocolate passion, he spent some years tinkering and tweaking before opening his small batch workshop in Columbia, Missouri in 2007. By 2008, Patric caught the attention of food critics and chocolate insiders; awards quickly followed, and have every year since. Patric does not operate a cafe or retail store, but sells to stores and online as they release new bars. Their selections include single origin, blended and flavored bars. Patric remains a small-scale operation, dedicated to meticulous, hand-made production. In addition, McClure offers consultancy services to those wishing to learn the chocolate craft. Sign up for their newsletter to hear of new chocolate releases at: patric-chocolate.com

RITUAL CHOCOLATE (USA)

"Small batch fine chocolate at 7,000 Ft," Ritual's website proclaims. Robbie Stout and Anna Davis operate a workshop and cafe in Park City, Utah. These owner- operators founded their company in 2010 and remain hands-on. Like a number of craft chocolate makers, a deep commitment to ecology and conservation informs their corporate values. Ritual produces a number of single origin bars featuring 75% cacao, blends and flavored bars of varying strengths, as well as drinking chocolate, spreads, and nibs. No need to ascend to higher altitude, you can purchase their delicious bars through many of the better chocolate retailers, as well as Ritual's online store: ritualchocolate.com

BAR AU CHOCOLAT (USA)

Nicole Trutanich founded Bar Au Chocolat in 2010. A boutique, small-batch producer, Ms. Trutanich takes a minimalist approach with just two ingredients– cacao and sugar. Her roasty notes are slightly contra-trend, refreshingly unique, and show off the classic flavors of each bean variety. I'm a big fan. Her bars work beautifully with and without whiskey. Bar Au Chocolat will be opening an atelier in Manhattan Beach, California in 2018. Can't wait! Meanwhile, order her bars from barauchocolat.com

CASTRONOVO CHOCOLATE (USA)

Owner-operator, Denise Castronovo, one of the top-rated bean-to-bar makers in the USA, earned more medals at the International Chocolate Awards than any other micro-batch producer in 2016. She has also earned awards from the Academy of Chocolate. In fact, Castronovo has not failed to take home a medal since 2014. She sources rare cacao beans from the indigenous people of the rainforests.

Castronovo has been crafting chocolate in her Stuart, Florida factory since 2013. Learn more at castronovochocolate.com

FRESCO ARTISAN CHOCOLATE (USA)

Fresco is a family-owned business, run by founders Rob and Amy Anderson. They commenced operations in 2010 and have been bringing awards home to northwest Washington State since 2012. I love the way they specify their roasting and conching characteristics on each bar! To find a store near you that carries their bars, or to buy from their online store go to frescochocolate.com

LETTERPRESS CHOCOLATE (USA)

Letterpress Chocolate is a small batch bean-to-bar chocolate maker based in Los Angeles. Founded in 2014 by David Menkes, owner and chocolate maker, and wife Corey Menkes, co-owner and CFO, Letterpress specializes in single-origin and special project bars. At the time of this writing, they were planning their first store. They pride themselves in forming direct relationships with farmers, paying them fair prices, and raising standards of living in the process. Letterpress won its first awards in 2017 for both their chocolate and packaging. To buy their bars, visit their website: letterpresschocolate.com

CHARM SCHOOL CHOCOLATE (USA)

Josh Rossen is an award-winning pastry chef who graduated from the Culinary Institute of America. He distinguished himself as Pastry Sous Chef at Mario Batali's Del Posto Restaurant in New York. After winning the Food Network's Sweet Genius Award in 2012, he opened his chocolate shop in Baltimore, Maryland. Charm School produces mostly flavored bars, but his award-winning Dark Belize 70% bar was included in this book and works beautifully with whiskeys. Try his other bars too! charmschoolchocolate.com

CREO CHOCOLATE (USA)

Award winning Creo specializes in bars made from Ecuadorian cacao beans. They operate a factory and cafe in Portland, Oregon that sells truffles and baked goods, as well as drinking chocolate. Visit their cafe if you're in the neighborhood, or order online at creochocolate.com

14

EASY-TO-MAKE WHISKEY TRUFFLES

There's nothing better than a good friend, except a good friend with chocolate.

— *Linda Grayson*

Those of you who read my previous book know that I began my journey as a chocolate enthusiast, reading whatever I could, then trained as a reviewer with Mark Christian of the C-spot®, where I still contribute occasional reviews to what, a decade later, remains the most influential chocolate review site on the web. In 2013, I found making truffles helped me through a family crisis. And while I never expected to actually make chocolate from bean-to-bar, I eventually tried that too. The chocolate bug doesn't bite everyone the way it bit me, but those of us who have been bitten will tell you that once cacao sinks her teeth into us, she has won, and the passion will run deep and lifelong.

Researching and writing takes an enormous amount of time, and during the most intense final months of that process, there isn't much opportunity to don my apron and do what I enjoy so much—coax shy flavors from their bean hiding places through roasting and refining, nor to watch rivulets of chocolate liquor emerge that I'll later hand-wrestle on a marble slab to rearrange its crystal formation—a process called tempering—to produce a gleaming, soul-invigorating-scented, deep brown pudding-like mixture that will set in a mold, and magically, transform into a glossy, hardened tablet. And it's been much too long since I've had the luxury to melt some of that chocolate, change it back into a liquidy form that I could use as a couverture—a coating for chocolate molds in order to make bonbons shells or chocolate bars. As I reach the end of this book, the thought of resuming these activities is a mouth-watering, heady promise of rejuvenation. How I look forward to every step, every aroma, every taste! And probably the first thing I'll do, once this book goes off to the publisher is reclaim my kitchen and whip up some whiskey truffles. Because first and foremost, flavor, taking it all in and creating it, is my heart beat.

You may be wondering, does the system I've been developing in this book for pairing flavor profiles of chocolate and whiskey work for making bonbons and truffles? Yes, it does! With some caveats. Pairing dark milk chocolate, regular milk chocolate, even white chocolate, by flavor conforms to this same method to the degree that there is any discernable profile. If you look at the few dark milk chocolates I've matched in this book, despite the small dairy component and increased sugar, you will see that if the profile was earthy, for example, it still worked with compatible whiskeys for that category. But as added milk and sugar, particularly in industrial milk and white chocolates, made from poorly flavored commodity beans, reduces flavors to just caramel, dairy, vanilla and sugar notes, you will have to find whiskeys that work with those limited flavor profiles. To the extent that the flavors of the cocoa mass are submerged and masked, it will be all about the whiskey. Flavor balances can easily shift. But if the milk chocolate coverture you want to use has caramel notes, you may find a few entries in my lists of pairings that might point you in the right direction.

You might think that a very sweet white chocolate would work with a contrasting strong whiskey, even a smoky one. But in the limited attempts I've made with industrial whites, that just tasted of sugar, sometimes vanilla, they were a disaster with peated, single malts which imparted any marine or medicinal notes. White chocolates did somewhat better with peated whiskies with no marine or medicinal notes, but still didn't garner my enthusiasm. Go for a dry, rather than sweet whiskey, sure, but watch those flavor notes! When using white chocolate in a bonbon or truffle, so much will depend on any flavors you may select in addition to the whiskey. There are too many variables you might choose to advise you specifically here, but I would suggest that if you're adding nuts, look for bars in my pairing lists that have nut notes, and see if that might give you a clue for a good whiskey companion. Do similarly when using citrusy (twang) or other fruits —look for bar pairings that reflect those profiles.

When making truffles or molded bonbons (pralines), alcohol proof and cacao content of the chocolate used in the ganache need to be carefully considered. Most scotch is only 80 proof. A few, like Macallan 12 Year are 86 proof. Use an 80 proof whisky (or whiskey) if making a ganache with a 68% or less cacao. If making a ganache with a cacao content of 68-70%, I recommend using a minimum of an 86 proof scotch or an American whiskey, most of which are 90 proof or higher. Bourbon works wonderfully in a ganache or with a shell in excess of 70%, but you will still have to find one from our list that has a compatible flavor profile.

If you've never tempered chocolate, there's never been a better time to learn at home. Why temper chocolate? Because it's beautiful, and shiny, it has snap when you break or bite it, and, relatively speaking, it somewhat preserves the chocolate and whatever it enrobes. It's fundamental for bonbon shells and coating truffles. That said, tempering is a skill that requires practice—a lot of it! And you will have to be mindful of room temperature and humidity, best under 70 F (21 C) and approximately 50% or less, respectively.

The simplest way to learn these days is to search for videos on YouTube, using the words: temper, chocolate. It's too tricky to learn from a book; you need to see the way a chocolatier works and how the chocolate reacts. Find a video of someone using the seeding method, with just chocolate and a microwavable plastic bowl (not glass, which retains too much heat). The chocolate couverture needs to be broken into small pieces. But some couverture producers save you the trouble with ready–to–use small discs or pistoles. Check the resource section of this book for a list of manufacturers of couverture. Do not use chocolate chips! They usually include ingredients that make them unsuitable.

The only reason to use 'couverture' chocolate is to achieve a less viscous, melted liquid that flows better when using it in molds. Otherwise, any tempered chocolate–including the bars listed in these pages, can be used for dipping and coating truffles. But you will still have to temper the chocolate after melting it.

To temper chocolate using the seeding method, as you will see in the YouTube videos, you will be, gently and slowly, melting the chocolate at a low setting of the microwave oven, beginning with 30 seconds, stir, then repeat if still solid, and once slightly softened, melt in the microwave in pulses of 10 second increments.

Pull it out frequently, stir it, repeat. When about 75 % is liquidy and there are still some chunks, you can remove the bowl and just stir until the chunks melt and cause the entire mixture to turn shiny. Or you can let the entire bowl of chocolate slowly and incrementally go liquidy—careful not to burn it!— then begin seeding it with unheated pieces to cool the temperature. When the chocolate becomes silky and shiny, it may signal that it has fallen into temper (crystallized in the correct way). Test it by dipping a butter knife or strip of parchment paper. Let the dipped item sit while you keep stirring. You will know within a few minutes whether the chocolate is in temper if it begins to harden, is shiny and doesn't produce streaks. The chocolate in the bowl will harden (in other words, it will set, right there in the bowl) if it sits too long, and you will have to learn how to maintain it at the right temperature to keep it workable. Light and brief use of a hairdryer on its lowest heat setting can help. Hold the blower, not too close to the surface of the chocolate, and gently blow across the surface for about 5-10 seconds. Stir the chocolate, test again with your knife or parchment strips. Keep stirring, and if the knife or the strips confirm that your chocolate is in temper, begin dipping your truffles. It's a bit of a tango, but it's my favorite dance.

You don't have to coat truffles with tempered chocolate. It holds them together nicely and stores best that way, and it adds a contrasting crunch to the buttery truffle ganache, but you can simply roll the truffles in cocoa powder, shredded coconut, or ground nuts—particularly if they will be consumed within a short period of time.

Here's a simple recipe for easy-to-make whiskey truffles. No tempering required.

If the chocolate you use is not listed in this book, first sample the chocolate and determine its dominant flavor profile. Check the manufacturer's website; sometimes they will give you information in their tasting notes. Find chocolates with similar flavor profiles in the book, then match the chocolate profile to a whiskey profile.

Again, you only need couverture chocolate if you're going to use molds. Couverture chocolate however is usually more economical if you're making large quantities. But for the truffles here, you can use any of the bars in this book. They should be fine for making truffle ganache for small recipes. However, you will need at least 3 bars, since most of them do not exceed 3 ounces. And some of the higher end bars can be costly x 3. Check the weight on the packages. Break them up in tiny pieces and weigh them to confirm that you have 8 ounces.

whiskey truffles

This recipe should make approximately 24 1/2-inch diameter truffles. Truffles work better if the ganache is slightly drier than that required when using a mold to create bonbons (pralines). If you are using this formulation for molded bonbons, you will need to increase the cream to 1/2 cup and up to 2 tablespoons of butter and whiskey, respectively.

ingredients:

8 ounces (226.8 grams) finely chopped chocolate
1/3 cup (2.667 fluid ounces, or 78.87 ml) heavy whipping cream
1¹/² tablespoons (21.191 gr) unsalted butter
1¹/² tablespoons (22.18 ml) whiskey
1 cup (64 g) unsweetened cocoa powder (or shredded coconut or ground nuts) for rolling truffles
Additional cocoa powder to coat your hands to prevent sticking while rolling the truffles.

equipment needed:

1. a kitchen scale
2. a firm, rubber spatula or shallow spoon
3. a medium-sized bowl for mixing the truffle ganache
4. a small sauce pan or microwavable plastic bowl
5. measuring cup
6. measuring spoons
7. plastic wrap
8. small melon ball scooper or two metal teaspoons
9. vinyl food preparers gloves
10. a shallow, square or rectangular pan
11. a cookie sheet or large flat plate or serving tray
12. wax-paper-lined cookie sheet, large flat plate or serving tray
13. a container in which to place the finished truffles

whiskey truffles

instructions:

prepare:
1. Set the butter out to soften to room temperature. Measure $1^{1/2}$ tablespoons and set it aside.
2. Measure out the $1^{1/2}$ tablespoons of whiskey into a small container or cup and set aside.
3. Pour the 1/3 cup of heavy whipping cream into the sauce pan or small microwavable bowl.
4. Place the 8 ounces of chocolate into the mixing bowl. Place the spatula or spoon next to the bowl.
5. Sprinkle at least half of the cocoa powder into the square or rectangular pan.

create the ganache:
1. Bring the cream to a scalding temperature, some bubbles just around the edge, but not to a full boil.
2. Remove the cream from stovetop or microwave.
3. Pour the cream over the chocolate and let it sit a few minutes.
4. Using the spatula, see if the chocolate is mostly soft, and blend the cream in, melting the rest of the chocolate. Work quickly to keep temperatures optimal.
5. Add the butter to the chocolate and cream mixture and stir thoroughly. The mixture should be reaching a pudding texture.
6. When fully blended, slowly add the whiskey and stir to

173

thoroughly distribute through the mixture.

7. Let it sit. Touch the bowl to see if it has achieved room temperature, or see if the mixture is stiffer (is setting).

8. Tear off a large piece of plastic wrap and push it down into the bowl so that it's lying on top of the mix. Smooth the wrap down all around the inside of the bowl so no air can get into the mixture.

9. Place the mixture into the refrigerator for about 1-2 hours.

make the truffles

1. When the mixture seems stiff throughout, it is ready to be removed for use.

2. Let the mixture sit until it softens just a little (otherwise, you will destroy your melon scooper and get crumbly ganache)

3. Scoop out the ganache using the melon scooper or teaspoons, and set each semi-sphere of ganache on the cookie sheet.

4. If they seem to be melting too much, you can refrigerate them a few minutes to make them firmer.

5. Put on the vinyl gloves or, with very clean, dry hands, sprinkle some cocoa powder on your palms and fingers and gently smooth the powder over them so they are lightly dusted.

6. Pick up a semi-sphere of ganache and quickly roll it with a circular motion between the fingers of both hands to form a smooth, rounded ball. Remember, the longer you roll them, the more they will melt. They don't have to be perfectly smooth. In fact the term truffle is because they resemble the truffle funghi. Place each rounded ball on the wax-paper- covered cookie sheet

7. Place the cookie sheet in the refrigerator for about ten

whiskey truffles

whiskey truffles

minutes to firm the ganache balls.

8. Remove the cookie sheet from the refrigerator, set it on your work space and let the ganache balls get just a tiny bit soft or tacky. If they get too soft, re-refrigerate them.

9. With fresh gloves, reapply cocoa powder on just your finger tips this time. Place the ganache balls one by one in the shallow square or rectangular pan containing the cocoa powder. If you're using another type coating, such as shredded coconut or ground nuts, you can place those into the shallow pan instead of the cocoa powder.

10. Move the pan gently back and forth and in a circular motion so that each ball rolls around in the cocoa powder, the coconut or the ground nuts. When fully coated, remove and place in the container you had set aside for the finished truffles.

11. Store the finished truffles in a cool environment. If you choose to refrigerate them, make sure the container is sealed and, to avoid condensation, don't open the lid until you wish to serve the truffles.

non-dairy or vegan substitutes

I find whiskey goes well with a creamy consistency of the dairy-based ganache, but some people must restrict milk products. If so, try to substitute one of these, following the same instructions as guidelines. You will need to experiment!

coconut-based ganache

Instead of dairy cream and butter, try 1/3 cup of coconut milk. Coconut oil and coconut butter usually smell strongly of coconut. So mind your flavor profiles! But if you want a more emollient consistency, you can add a teaspoon of coconut oil or coconut butter. Coconut butter can have a fibrous texture, however, so you'll have to experiment to see if you like it. I suggest using only 1 tablespoon of whiskey for a full recipe of the coconut milk based truffle. Eight full ounces of chocolate might seem a lot to waste if you don't like the results. Therefore, before committing to a full 8 ounces of chocolate, you might try cutting the recipe. Taste to see how you like the combination of the whiskey, the coconut and the chocolate

water ganache

Water ganaches have become all the rage for those who prefer more naked flavors of the chocolate and a lighter, cleaner consistency. Instead of using coconut, you can try making a water ganache, substituting hot water for cream and butter. The texture will be less emollient, but you may like it. While it won't quiet some of the spectrum of the whiskey flavors as much as the dairy-based cream and butter, it may work well with a mild whiskey. I recommend starting out using only 1 tablespoon of an 80 proof scotch for a full recipe using water ganache. Remember, you need to use less water because you are substituting that tablespoon of whiskey for an equivalent amount of water. You might begin with a half recipe just to test whether you like a water ganache. When you pour the hot water into the chocolate, begin stirring immediately. Once the chocolate and water have blended smoothly, add the whiskey at the very last and blend it in well. See if this combination appeals to your palate.

Enjoy!

whiskey truffles

ACKNOWLEDGEMENTS

As I began this journey in whiskey a complete novice, I am indebted to the many writers, educators, distillers, sales representatives, spirits ambassadors, and retailers who taught me so much, so quickly. Translating tasting skills from chocolate to whiskey required study and a whole lot of practice. In particular, special thanks go to Carlos Abeyta, former Ambassador of Bruichladdich, the Astor Center of New York City, and The Flatiron Room of New York City

I could not have compiled tasting data without the generosity of Steve Hawley of Westland Distillery, David de Fazio and Jessica Spalding of Wyoming Whiskey, Lenny Eckstein of Deerhammer Distilling Company, Ralph Erenzo of Tuthillown Spirits, John Weiss and Alessandra Carriero of Curich Weiss, William Grant & Sons, Jason Moore and Nathalie Sinclair of Whyte & Mackay Americas, and Allison Parc of Brenne French Single Malt Whisky. Special thanks to retailers Jack Battipaglia of Gotham Wine and Spirits and the staff at Gramercy Wine and Spirits for treating me like an insider.

Publishing my Deep Tasting series would be impossible without the talents and support of Publisher, Catherine Lewis of Ritual Communications; Editor, Janie Dullard of Lector's Books, and my book designer, Lisa Hayden-Miller of Photomagic Designs. Lisa, the cover you created says it all!

Love and gratitude go to my Interfaith community and dear friends in the chocolate world, including, Mark Christian of the C-spot®, the Well-Tempered group, my chocolate alma mater Ecole Chocolat, and The Fine Chocolate Industry Association.

John, you and our tiny angel, Rhonda, are always the wind under my chocolate wings.

REFERENCES

BOOKS

David Broom. The World Atlas of Whisky. 2nd Edition. Mitchell Beazley. 2014

Michael Jackson, Dominic Roskrow, Gavin D. Smith, William C. Meyers. Michael Jackson's Complete Guide to Single Malt Scotch. Doris Kindersley Ltd. Sixth Edition. 2010

Cyrille Mald, Alexandre Vingtier. Iconic Whisky. Jacqui Small LLP. 2016. Translated from the French edition, 2015, by Anne Mc Dowall.

R. M. Peluso. Deep Tasting: A Chocolate Lover's Guide to Meditation. Ritual Communications. 2016.

Maricel E. Presilla. The New Taste of Chocolate; A Cultural & Natural History of Cacao with Recipes. Ten Speed Press. 2001.

David Wishart. Whisky Classified: Choosing Single Malts by Flavour. 10th Anniversary Edition. Pavilion Books LTD. 2012.

eBOOKS

Dave Broom. Whisky: The Manual. Mitchell Beazley. 2014

Lew Bryson. Tasting Whiskey: An Insider's Guide to the Unique Pleasures of the World's Finest Spirits. Storey Publishing. 2014.

Heather Greene. Whiskey Distilled: A Populist Guide to the Water of Life. Avery. 2014

Davin de Kergommeaux. Canadian Whisky: the Portable Expert. McClelland &Stewart. 2012.

Fred Minnick. Bourbon: The Rise, Fall, and Rebirth of an American Whiskey. Voyageur Press. 2016.

Fred Minnick. Bourbon Curious: A Simple Tasting Guide for the Savvy Drinker. Zenith Press.2015.

Fred Minnick. Whiskey Women. Potamac Books. 2013

ARTICLES

A. C. Aprotosoaie, S. V. Luca, A. Miron. "Flavor Chemistry of Cocoa and Cocoa Products—An Overview." Comprehensive Reviews in Food Science and Food Safety. (2016).15: 73–91. doi:10.1111/1541-4337.12180.

Karen Best. "Do Whiskey's Legs Matter?" The Whiskey Wash (online). thewhiskeywash.com
May 2, 2017

Monike Buczek. "Chocolate: The Fermentation and Flavors of the Chocomicrobiome." Microbial Sciences. (online) ASM.org
30 March 2017

Shauncy Ferro. "Your Complete Guide to Chocolate Flavors," Popular Science (online), March 15, 2013, with Infographics by Sean Seidell.

Yuri Kageyama. "Japan one-ups Scotch with whisky, coveted around the world." The News- Herald (online). March 18, 2017.

K.-Y. Lee, A. Paterson, J. Piggott, G. Richardson.
"Origins of Flavour in Whiskies and a Revised Flavour Wheel: a Review"
Journal of the Institute of Brewing. (2001)Volume 107, No. 5, pp.287-313.

Carla Martin. "Sizing the craft chocolate market," Fine Cacao and Chocolate Institute (blog), August 31, 2017,
https://chocolateinstitute.org/blog/sizing-the-craft-chocolate-market

Jonny McCormick. "Peat Wave." Whisky Advocate. Summer 2017. Pp.106-110.

Beverly Merz. "This is your brain on alcohol." Harvard Health Publications (online).July14, 2017.
www.health.harvard.edu/blog/this-is-your-brain-on-alcohol

Fred Minnick "Barreling Ahead: Whiskey-Making Break Cherished Traditions to Create New Flavors" Scientific American. (online) The Sciences. March 14, 2013.

Travis Mitchell "The Future of Craft Whiskey According to the Innovative Tuthilltown Spirits." Paste Quarterly (online) pastemagazine.com. February 9, 2017.

Research we're watching. "Alcohol's heart advantages under scrutiny." Harvard Health Letter (online) August 1, 2017.
www.health.harvard.edu/heart-health/alcohols-heart- advantages-under-scrutiny

The Whisky Professor "The Importance of Water." scotchwhisky.com January, 18, 2016

PERIODICALS
Whisky Advocate Magazine

Artisan Spirit Magazine,
the endorsed publication of the American Craft Spirits Association

WEBSITES
The C-spot ® c-spot.com

canadianwhisky.org

distiller.com

Selfbuilt's whiskyanalysis.com

whiskymagazine.com

RESOURCES

DNA testing can be obtained through a number of services these days, but be sure you get the full and accurate picture through a qualified genetic counselor. Without such counseling, misinterpretations can be devastating. Good counseling should include education and options. Interpretation of testing results should be provided by someone certified by the American Board of Medical Genetics (www.abmgg.org) or the American Board of Genetic Counseling (www.abgc.net)

Alcoholics Anonymous: https://www.aa.org

Al-Anon, support for families and friends of alcoholics: https://al-anon.org

Overeater's Anonymous: https://oa.org

EDUCATION SPONSORED BY THE SPIRITS INDUSTRY
The Foundation for Advancing Alcohol Responsibility:
https://www.responsibility.org

The Distilled Spirits Council of the United States discus.org

The Scotch Whisky Association scotch-whisky.org.uk

COUVERTURE CHOCOLATE

Couverture chocolate is designed for enrobing, dipping and use in molds. Not all chocolate designed to enrobe and dip is suitable for use in molds. Only couverture which flows easily and has less viscosity is appropriate for that purpose. Ask about use when contacting the company. If you don't see a favorite craft bar brand here, call the company. If they make bonbons or truffles for their store or cafe, they may make couverture. Ask if you can purchase some. Some will custom design.

COCOA BARRY (SUBSIDIARY OF BARRY CALLEBAUT)

I have no experience with this product. Contact the company for information. cacao- barry.com

DIVINE CHOCOLATE (GERMANY, WIDELY DISTRIBUTED IN THE USA)

I have no personal experience using their couverture. divinechocolate.com

EL REY CHOCOLATE (VENEZUELAN, DISTRIBUTED IN THE USA)

Award winning maker of Icoa white chocolate, other milks and dark chocolates designed as couverture and eating bars. I have personally used their couverture and it is good quality at a reasonable price. They designate their bars for specific use. Given the geopolitical situation in Venezuela, I contacted their USA distributor. They told me their product continues to be made and shipped to the USA. chocolates-elrey.com

FRUITION CHOCOLATE

This is an independent craft chocolate maker. Their Hispaniola 68% bar is couverture. It is used extensively in-house, where I have tasted it and worked with it. It's of very good quality. Contact Fruition to ask about options for couverture bars. tastefruition.com

GUITTARD (USA)

Fifth generation, independent chocolate producer. I have tasted many of their bars and sampled their couverture, but have not worked with it. However, they have a long history of producing couverture that is widely accepted for all purposes. Guittard has good quality products and is a reliable company.
guittard.com

MADÉCASSE (MADAGASCAR/USA)

Madécasse makes couverture discs, but I have no experience using them. Contact the company for information on intended use.
madecasse.com

VALRHONA (FRANCE, DISTRIBUTED IN THE USA)

Excellent quality couvertures, for all uses, but pricey.
valrhona-chocolate.com

ABOUT THE AUTHOR

Reverend Dr. R. M. Peluso, a graduate of Columbia University and The New Seminary, is an ordained Interfaith minister who has practiced meditation for over four decades. A chocolate reviewer for the C-spot® since its inception, she founded Chocolate Tasting Meditation™ in 2006. Dr. Peluso studied chocolate making with Ecole Chocolat and creates chocolate from bean-to-bonbons... just for the love of it. She is author of the Deep Tasting Guide™ series, which includes book one, *Deep Tasting: A Chocolate Lover's Guide to Meditation*. *Deep Tasting Chocolate & Whiskey* is the second in the series.

Dr. Peluso is available for speaking engagements, interviews and guest blogging. Email her at **revrmpeluso@gmail.com**

Are you planning a conference, meeting, party or fund raising event? Are you a spiritual community interesting in introducing your congregation to meditation? Reverend Dr. R. M. Peluso will be happy to lead your group in guided tastings or tasting meditations. Find out more by contacting Dr. Peluso through the **ctm-chocolate-tasting-meditation.com** website or by email at **revrmpeluso@gmail.com**

www.ingramcontent.com/pod-product-compliance
Lightning Source LLC
Chambersburg PA
CBHW070051120426
42742CB00048B/2013